ERIE LACKAWANNA

Memories

THE FINAL YEARS

Preston Cook

Erie Lackawanna Memories
The Final Years
by Preston Cook

copyright © 1987

First Edition
Manufactured in the United States of America

For information write to:
Old Line Graphics
1604 Woodwell Road
Silver Spring, Maryland 20906

Layout and Design by: D.A. McFall
Typesetting by: Graphic World, Inc., Rockville, MD
Printed by: French/Bray, Inc., Glen Burnie, MD

Library of Congress Catalog Card Number 87-61476

TABLE OF CONTENTS

This book is dedicated to
the people who worked for the
Erie Lackawanna

ACKNOWLEDGEMENTS

Many people contributed information and material which I collected over the years and applied in this book. In particular I would like to acknowledge the assistance of Jim Boyd, Larry DeYoung, Roger Rasor, Charles ("Sandy") Burton, Dave McWherter, Joe Slanser, Don Dover, and Dan Dover for their help and guidance.

The audience was completely captivated as the images paraded across the screen. E-units hammering the diamond at Marion to a soundtrack of a Sousa march ... an RS3 silhouetted in the nocturnal fog to the haunting beat of a contemporary movie theme ... a quintette of Alcos belching smoke to the cannonades of the "1812 Overture." Preston Cook was putting on his automated audio/visual "Erie Lackawanna Show" for the Jersey Central Chapter NRHS.

These slides were far too good to be enjoyed by only the select few who were fortunate enough to be within reach of a railroad club show. I had been trying to interest Preston in doing a book for some time, but the right combination of publisher and layout artist never quite seemed to come together. Never, that is, until I learned that Don McFall was looking for material for a full color book. It is with considerable pride that I can say that I suggested Cook to McFall and McFall to Cook. You hold the results in your hands.

With this book, the fleeting images of the screen can linger forever, though you'll have to fill in your own soundtrack. The chapters in this book approximate the arrangement of that slide show, although there have been some changes and additions to make the subject matter better suit the printed page. But the color, the drama and impact of Preston's coverage of the Erie Lackawanna comes through undiminished.

Preston Cook is a fascinating individual on several counts. He is first-off an Erie Lackawanna fan. Not an Erie fan and not a Lackawanna fan, but a true ERIE LACKAWANNA fan. He has covered the system from Chicago to Hoboken and knows it from operation to motive power and from gondola car lettering details to the delicate colors of the Canisteo Valley in the morning mists. He has the technical knowledge of a professional railroader combined with the sensitive eye of an accomplished photographer. His enthusiasm for the EL is infectious.

Preston's photography is an unusual mix of rigid conservatism and stunning artistic insight. While he demands nearly perfect lighting conditions for daytime photography — I doubt you'll find more than a handful of cloudy-day shots in this entire book — he is quick to recognize and capture the particular charm of sunsets and fog and the unlimited mysteries of the night. While a dull gray overcast will keep the cameras in the car and send him to the laundromat with a good book, a rainy night will find him protecting the cameras with an umbrella while splashing around a muddy railroad yard madly throwing flashbulb bursts into the gloom. He loves the extremes, sunlight and dark, but cannot abide with a grubby day.

This book and his slide show are typical of Preston's approach to the hobby. He limits his topics to those things in which he is truly interested and then dives in to a depth few would truly understand. (Take diesel locomotive drawings, for instance, as in "plans" in model railroad magazines. Over the past decade Preston almost singlehandedly set a new level of standards for published plans of diesel locomotives. No longer would it be acceptable to simply copy the inaccurate "general arrangement drawings" supplied by the manufacturers. Preston set a new level of accuracy with carefully photo-documented studies that acknowledged all the variations and invariably showed both sides in full detail.) His audio/visual Erie Lackawanna slide show demonstrated an early understanding and mastery of the art. With the logic of an engineer he defined the project, evaluated the available equipment and put the whole package together in a remarkably short time—and then went on to describe the whole process in guest CAMERA BAG columns in the May and July 1986 RAILFAN & RAILROAD.

To me, the Erie Lackawanna was one of the more interesting railroads that came into Chicago, where I did much of my early railfanning in the 1960s. In 1971 I moved to New Jersey and lived and worked within earshot of the old Erie mainline. In between, I photographed the EL pretty much from end to end. I saw the U25Bs in factory-fresh paint at State Line Tower and watched the endless parades of "3600s" howling through Ramsey and Suffern. I know the sound of E8s urging a mile of dead freight out of Huntington, Indiana, and the chant of F-units on the "Bloom."

And I know what Marion, Ohio looked like at night and how the Dayton train see-sawed through town. But I was only in Marion on one or two occasions and don't recall ever taking a night shot there. "My" Marion memories are through Preston Cook's slides seen in numerous railfan gatherings over the years. My Erie Lackawanna memories are more extensive than my personal experiences, thanks to Preston Cook.

May this book do the same for you.

Jim Boyd
Newton, New Jersey
May 22, 1987

PERSPECTIVE

I don't have a favorite railroad, but if I did, the Erie Lackawanna would be near the top of the list. Most of my photography of the EL was done in a short two and one half year span between February 1972 and October 1974, when I lived in Marion, Ohio. This book is a personal photo album of my favorite shots from that period. In a few instances, where the scope of the coverage or the interest of the subject matter dictated, material has been used which was taken at the end of the Erie Lackawanna's sixteen year life in 1976, or in the early years of the Conrail era.

My style of photography and preferences in subject matter and composition were heavily influenced by my early experiences as a railroad enthusiast, living in New England. In my Junior year of high school, I was fortunate to participate in the Honeywell "Science All Stars" television show with a science project which I had taken to the state and national science fairs, and my appearence on the series brought with it a Pentax H1A camera provided by the sponsor. This was an unusually fine piece of photographic equipment for a sixteen year old to have, and I quickly found uses for my new camera, concentrating on two local subjects which I found to be of greatest interest; the New Haven railroad and the marine industry. At that time, I had no idea there were other railfans in the world, or other marine enthusiasts. This may have been a positive influence in the development of my preferences in photography, as I was able to avoid from the beginning the

"baseball card" approach of repetitive three quarter view roster shooting that tends to be overly dominant in the railroad hobby. I made no deliberate effort to take three quarter views, quite simply because I didn't know what they were, and I began shooting night scenes almost immediately because nobody told me there was anything unusual about that type of photography. Since I had no way of knowing that locomotives were the preferred subject of the vast majority of rail photographers, freight cars and cabooses were treated as equal opportunity targets in my early photography, and have received a major part of my attention in the years since.

Most of my photography during high school was done using the exposure instructions which came with the film, since I didn't have an exposure meter until sometime after developing an interest in rail photography. Fortunately, I began shooting Kodachrome film almost from the beginning, which saved me the agony experienced by many railfans who have watched their slides, shot on other types of film, turn different colors or fade out completely with age. I never found the time to take a course in photography, though I would have liked to, and most of the learning process during the last two years of high school was by trial and error. During that time I wasn't shooting very memorable material, but I kept notes and tried to learn from my errors. That first 35mm camera, which I occasionally use to this day, and the ample collection of "mis-kes" I generated in the self-taught learning process, provided valuable training which I eventually was able to take advantage of in later years. My original H1A Pentax and its standard 55mm f2.0 lens were used for most of the photographs which appear in this book.

When the New Haven became part of the Penn Central, I was in college studying mechanical engineering, and the speed with which the railroad was absorbed and the rapid disappearance of its motive power and rolling stock left a lasting impression. When I graduated, my career involved a relocation to Marion, Ohio, a medium sized city located about fifty miles north of Columbus, and the location of major shop facilities on the Erie Lackawanna Railroad. Prior to my move to Marion, I shared the contemporary eastern rail enthusiasts view of the Erie Lackawanna (that the world is flat and the EL falls off the edge just west of Binghamton, New York). There were stories of operations in Meadville, Buffalo, Youngstown, Akron, Marion and Chicago, and I had even seen a few published photographs to provide confirmation, but all those places were incredibly remote from New England.

When I arrived in Marion, in February 1972, I found that the Erie Lackawanna Railroad was the dominating industry in the town, the area's largest employer and source of financial support and tax revenue, as well as a constant presence through the frequent movement of its trains across the town's many grade crossings. The EL provided a better opportunity than I had ever previously had to observe, close up, the operation of a class one railroad.

There were four major railroads operating through Marion, but the EL, with its colorful grey, maroon, and yellow paint scheme inherited from the Lackawanna, made a far more impressive showing than the drab blue or black units of the Norfolk & Western, the pseudo-black of the Penn Central (the mix ratio was about 10 parts of the black paint to one part green), or the blue pre-safety scheme units of the Chesapeake & Ohio. The Erie Lackawanna's Marion Diesel Shop personnel were friendly and photographic releases were readily available for rail enthusiasts interested in the operations on the railroad. It was even possible at the time, through the railroad's public relations staff, to sign a release and ride either the locomotives or the caboose of any train operating on the railroad.

Unfortunately, the Erie Lackawanna's Alco FAs and PAs had gone to trade several years before my arrival in Ohio, but there were plenty of other subjects of interest to photograph on the railroad. The fleet of EMD E8 cab units, which had been re-geared for freight service after the demise of the road's last through passenger trains (the LAKE CITIES in 1970), were always a favorite subject, the elderly EMD F7s

were abundant in the operations around Marion, and the Alco RS3 roadswitchers with their smoky 244 prime movers always put on a good show while switching the yards.

The area around the Marion Diesel Shop was well lit at night, with numerous tungsten spotlights on the shop buildings and on light towers around the yard. I began experimenting with films and filter combinations to obtain the most pleasing results with the available lighting, and eventually determined that Kodachrome II used with an 80C blue filter and a slight color correction magenta filter sheet provided almost the same lighting effects under the shop lights as was obtained with sunlight. The same basic color filter combination was used for hundreds of night shots at the Marion Shops, with the exposures bracketed at 30 seconds, one minute, and two minutes at f5.6. Occasionally, when a locomotive was in an area where the shop lighting was not adequate, I would obtain some additional lighting by aiming the automobile headlights at the unit, or by using clear flashbulbs in a press-type flash gun, set off manually while the camera shutter was open during the time exposure. This technique of "color painting" with flash was also useful in situations where there was very little available light, and most of the photographs taken at Gladstone, New Jersey, were done with open shutter flash, walking around the trains and setting off #2 flashbulbs at regular intervals for illumination.

The brief span of my two and one half years in Marion saw the demise of the few remaining Baldwins which had been inherited from the Erie, the retirement of a major portion of the road's Alco switcher fleet, the delivery of SD45-2s from EMD and U36Cs from GE, and the chaotic decline of the Erie Lackawanna into bankruptcy and reorganization from which it never recovered. The period from 1972-1974 on which most of the material in this book is based, was one of the most interesting times in the short, exciting life of this fascinating railroad. The events that were the subjects of my photography seem like they just happened yesterday, although it was more than fifteen years ago.

INTRODUCTION

This book is intended to be a celebration of the color and the excitement of the short, precarious existence of a fascinating railroad. The Erie Lackawanna Railroad started out with expectations of permanence, but was unable to maintain a financially secure position in the railroad industry. In the spring of 1976, as America was approaching the celebration of its 200th birthday, the Erie Lackawanna had reached the proverbial "end of the line" at fifteen years of age.

The Erie Lackawanna Railroad was the product of the October 17, 1960 merger of the Erie Railroad and the Delaware, Lackawanna & Western. The "Friendly Service Route" connected New York, Buffalo, Cleveland, and Chicago, crossing the Southern Tier of New York state, portions of Pennsylvania and New Jersey, and the industrial and agricultural areas of Ohio and Indiana. The short but exciting life of the Erie Lackawanna included operation as an independent railroad, control by the Norfolk & Western's Dereco holding company (of which the neighboring Delaware & Hudson was also a part), financial failure and bankruptcy followed by an unsuccessful attempt at reorganization, and the eventual inclusion of major segments of the railroad in the government-sponsored Conrail Corporation.

The Erie Lackawanna found itself in the midst of an uphill fight to maintain financial solvency almost from the moment it was created. The merger of the Erie Railroad and the Delaware, Lackawanna & Western

had been intended to enhance the chances of profitable operation of major portions of both predecessors property, through the economies of operation which could be realized by elimination of the duplicate services and parallel trackage which existed over some portions of the predecessor road's systems. In 1957 the Interstate Commerce Commission had authorized the Lackawanna to operate their trains between Binghamton and Corning, New York, over the Erie Railroad mainline, in order to allow both railroads to realize some financial advantage through the elimination of many miles of duplicate double-track mainline. Consequently, most of the Lackawanna main between these two cities had been eliminated around the time of the Erie Lackawanna merger. Following the 1960 merger, the respective Erie and Lackawanna trackage east of Binghamton, New York, remained as it had been. The former Lackawanna mainline between Corning and Buffalo was downgraded, first to local service, and finally became two branch lines through the elimination of about twenty miles of track, between Wayland and Mt. Morris, New York, in its midsection.

Unfortunately, both predecessor roads brought heavy debt loads into the merger, and the savings sought through the elimination of redundant facilities and operations still did not generate a financially healthy railroad. The merger of the Pennsylvania Railroad and the New York Central to create the Penn Central further endangered the Erie Lackawanna. As the consequence of an extremely complex series of negotiations and lawsuits, and as the result of an ICC order, the EL and the D&H were absorbed in 1968 by Dereco, a holding company owned by the Norfolk & Western. This arrangement provided some shelter for the financially strained EL, although there were few outward signs of changes resulting from the railroad's inclusion in Dereco. In conjunction with the Dereco inclusion, the railroad's official name was changed from the Erie Lackawanna RAILROAD to the Erie Lackawanna RAILWAY.

A major setback for the Erie Lackwanna was the 1969 inclusion of the New Haven Railroad in the Penn Central merger. The Erie Lackawanna had shared a substantial level of traffic flow with the New Haven, which was interchanged at the New Haven's yard in Maybrook, New York from a connection with the former Erie mainline at Campbell Hall, New York. When the New Haven became part of a competitive system rather than a friendly interchange partner, most of the traffic through the Maybrook interchange evaporated. With increasing operating expenses and declining traffic in many markets, the railroad faced an increasingly tougher challenge to stay profitable.

When I arrived in Ohio in 1972 as the representative of a railroad equipment supplier, the EL was already operating under severe financial restraints. Maintenance and operating budgets were tightly controlled, and substantial reductions in personnel had been adopted in an attempt to keep the railroad solvent. Faced with the certainty that the heavy industrial base in the Northeast would continue to decline, with a resultant reduction in the need for heavy rail transportation, and challenged by stiff competition from both the Penn Central and the trucking industry, the Erie Lackawanna operated along a narrow boundary between solvency and bankruptcy. The bankruptcy of the EL's competitor and interchange partner Penn Central contributed little to the Erie Lackawanna's traffic but saddled the railroad with an additional financial burden since the Penn Central was able to defer payment of debts owed the marginally solvent EL from the interchange of traffic between the two railroads. Although many other factors also contributed to the demise of the Erie Lackawanna, the Penn Central bankruptcy had a destabilizing effect on all of its weaker interchange partners in the Northeast, setting the stage for a string of financial failures among railroads in the region. By the early 1970's, the Lehigh Valley, the Central Railroad of New Jersey, the Lehigh & Hudson River, and the Reading Company were all involved in bankruptcy proceedings. The chaotic situation in the region eventually prompted Congress to seek a solution by authorizing the United States Railway Administration (USRA) to develop a plan for consolidation of the many bankrupt lines in the northeast. The USRA study of the problem resulted in the formation of the Consolidated Railroads Corporation (Conrail) in 1976.

The bankruptcy of the Erie Lackawanna had been a threat since the loss of the New Haven interchange traffic, but the issue was finally decided by the extensive damage caused by Hurricane Agnes in 1972. The hurricane washed out miles of the Erie Lackawanna mainlines in the Canisteo River Valley of south central New York state, requiring expensive repairs to the roadbed and detour movement of EL traffic over competitive lines in the United States and Canada. The total damages to the physical plant of the railroad as a result of flooding exceeded $4.9 million, while the revenue losses and the cost of detour moves ran the operating expenses of the railroad up over the $11 million mark. More than 300 miles of the railroad were put out of service as a result of the flooding, which also damaged four locomotives and more than 700 freight cars. In addition, the railroad's structures and lineside electrical equipment were also damaged extensively. By the time it was all over, the total cost of Hurricane Agnes to the Erie Lackawanna had exceeded $20 million, forcing the railroad into bankruptcy.

Two trustees, Cleveland businessmen Ralph S. Tyler, Jr. and Thomas F. Patton, were appointed to manage the company's affairs during reorganization. Working with Erie Lackawanna President Gregory W. Maxwell and the administration of the railroad, they attempted to put together a viable plan to restore financial solvency to the troubled company. Studies of the traffic and the railroad's physical plant resulted in the implimentation of several drastic measures to further reduce duplicate track mileage and reduce maintenance costs. Included in this program was the single-tracking of much of the former Erie Railroad mainline between Binghamton and Port Jervis, New York, and some reductions in branchline mileage. The track removed from the former Erie mainline was to be salvaged for use in the 1973 and 1974 track maintenance programs on other areas of the railroad, thus reducing the expense of the program work for the two year period. The former Delaware, Lackawanna & Western mainline through Scranton, Pennsylvania was to be upgraded and the overhead clearances increased to compensate for the reductions being made to the capabilities of the Erie line. In addition, new purchases of locomotives and rolling stock were planned to update the railroad's motive power and revenue equipment fleets.

In a hearing of the bankruptcy court in March, 1973, the trustees reorganization plan was accepted and the railroad was authorized to reorganize on an income basis with a completion date of 1981. Since the reorganization of the railroad seemed, at the time, to be a reasonable and feasible plan and an attainable goal, there was no intention for the Erie Lackawanna to be included with the other regional bankrupt lines in the USRA plans for consolidation of the bankrupts. However, the railroad's financial performance in 1973 and 1974 turned out to be disappointing, and when the national economy suffered a downturn and it became clear that the EL's 1975 financial performance was going to be unsatisfactory, the railroad's situation became critical, and the modernization programs were trimmed back (including the last minute cancellation of locomotive orders for 19 GP38-2s from the Electro-Motive Division of General Motors and for 20 U23Bs from General Electric Corporation). Since there seemed to be little prospect of the successful reorganization of the railroad within the court-specified time period, the decision was reached by the management and the trustees to petition for the inclusion of the Erie Lackawanna in the government sponsored Conrail (Consolidated Railroads) plan which would combine all the bankrupt lines in the northeast under a single system.

In July of 1975, the USRA issued their final system plan for the creation of Conrail, which included the Erie Lackawanna as a component of a system which would also encompass the Penn Central, the Reading, the Lehigh Valley, the Central of New Jersey, and the Lehigh & Hudson River Railroads. The plan called for the creation of Conrail on April 1, 1976. After considerable discussion, a last minute bid by the Chessie System to purchase portions of the Erie Lackawanna and the Reading failed to materialize, and at 11:59 PM EST on March 31, 1976 the Erie Lackawanna became a part of Conrail and of history.

Following the railroad's inclusion in Conrail, the end came quickly for many parts of the Erie Lackawanna system, as portions of the line and many of the railroad's shops and support facilities were redundant in the Conrail System. In the years since, many miles of the railroad's former right-of-way, as well as its yards and locomotive servicing terminals, have been abandoned and scrapped. Across much of Ohio and Indiana, the legacy of the Erie Lackawanna is a weed-infested trail of crushed stone ballast, stripped of its rails, rapidly being overgrown by trees, and barely discernable from the ground or the air.

Now that you know the ending, let me take you back to the days when the future still seemed to hold some promise for the "Friendly Service Route", and the "end of the line" was not yet in sight. In the early 1970s, the "west end" of the Erie Lackawanna saw lots of heavy freight traffic. The yards and engine facility at Marion, Ohio were scenes of constant activity, and a fascinating assortment of "first generation" diesels powered the Dayton trains and the Ashland turns. On the "east end" the railroad still operated elderly electric multiple unit cars hauling commuters on quaint branches through the New Jersey countryside, while the latest locomotive models powered heavy trains of UPS trailers on demanding schedules. Let me share with you some memories of the final years of the Erie Lackawanna, in the days when there was plenty of exciting action to be seen and photographed on this colorful railroad.

Preston Cook
1987

Chapter 1   MARION, OHIO AND THE WEST END

The west end of the Erie Lackawanna could be a very busy place at times. Although the actual western terminus of the railroad was at 51st Street Yard in Chicago, much of the motive power on the west end, as well as many of the symbol trains, operated from the Erie Lackawanna's extensive yard complex in Marion, Ohio. Through van trains, expedited merchandise service, and a substantial number of general freight trains operated between the Marion Yards and interchange connections in Chicago. Trains arriving in Marion from the east end, and traffic from the local Marion interchanges with the Chesapeake & Ohio and the Norfolk & Western, were flat switched or run over the hump yard to be pre-blocked for movement to the westbound interchange destinations. These movements of auto parts, heavy machinery, and general merchandise constituted the many sections of trains 97 and 99, and could be destined for any of the Erie Lackawanna's principal Chicago area interchange partners: the IHB yards at Riverdale, the Belt Railway yard at Summit, the Santa Fe at Corwith, the Burlington Northern at Clyde, the Chicago & North Western at Proviso, or the Milwaukee Road at Bensenville.

The opposite movement of freight from the connections in Chicago to Marion for blocking to destinations in the east comprised the numerous sections of trains 98 and 100. Depending on the priority of the cargo and the available locomotives in Chicago, the power on these trains could be anything from elderly

Electro-Motive E8s and F7s to modern SD45s and General Electric U36Cs. During the grain harvest season, large cuts of covered hoppers were frequently added to the usual fare of merchandise laden boxcars, gondolas transporting steel pipe, plates, and slabs, flats loaded with machinery, transformers, and farm tractors, and tank cars carrying chemicals, fuel, and other liquid cargo.

Marion was the hub of much of the activity on the west end of the Erie Lackawanna, and the location of the "running" diesel shop which maintained many of the units assigned to road service as well as the switching power which handled local industry and the branch line operations. The Marion diesel shop had been built in the 1950s to a standard EMD originated design, and was located next to the site of the steam roundhouse. The shop was equipped to handle all the running maintenance and periodic inspections of the locomotives based there, and was capable of handling changes of trucks, traction motors, diesel engine turbochargers, and locomotive main generators. While the Marion facility could handle the overhaul of diesel locomotive prime movers, that work was usually left to the railroad's heavy repair shop at Hornell, New York, which also did the carbody refurbishing and repainting work on the railroad's locomotive fleet. The motive power assigned at Marion included all of the EMD SD45s, SDP 45s, and the GP35s. A large group of the streamlined EMD E8s, which were converted to freight service gearing after the demise of the railroad's through passenger trains, were also based here, and a substantial portion of the 1950s vintage EMD F7 road unit fleet also called Marion home. The EMD GP7s and GP9s, as well as the EMD switchers, were not often seen at Marion in the 1970s, being primarily assigned to the shops on the east end of the railroad for maintenance. Alco power was abundant at Marion, with all of the Century 425s being assigned there, (the Century 424s were maintained by Youngstown at the time), and the shop also maintained the 1000-class RS3s which handled local switching and branchline work, and a portion of the remaining Alco S2 switchers. General Electric locomotives maintained by the Marion shops included the U25Bs, the U33Cs, and the U36Cs, while the U34CH commuter units were maintained on the east end of the railroad.

The engine facility at Marion was located on the northeast corner of the Erie Lackawanna's freight yards, and just to the east of the yards the EL and Penn Central jointly shared tracks that crossed the interlocking plant at Marion Tower (called "AC" tower in the 1970s). At this point the joint tracks (running almost due east and west) consisted of an eastbound and a westbound mainline, with a lead into the EL yard as a third track on the north side of the mainlines. The tower was located on the north side of the tracks while the Marion Union Depot stood on the south side of the tracks. The depot had been inactive for several years, but the former bunkhouse was occupied by the Marion Model Railroad Club. Just to the west of the tower and depot the two track mainline of the Chesapeake & Ohio crossed the EL/PC tracks, and to the east of the tower (right at the foot of the tower stairs) the two track Norfolk & Western (formerly Pennsylvania Railroad) mainline crossed the combined Erie Lackawanna and Penn Central tracks, running along the east side of the Erie Lackawanna office building next to the depot. In the early 1970s the interlocking plant frequently had more traffic than it could handle efficiently, with as many as one hundred moves across the plant in a twenty-four hour period. The greatest traffic density I was able to confirm during my stay in Marion was 124 moves in one day.

Marion was the originating yard for the interesting trains of the Dayton Branch, with train MD97 operating westbound from Marion to Dayton daily, and train DM98 making the opposite trip each day. The Dayton trains had to back eastward from the Marion yard through the AC interlocking plant, crossing the C&O and the N&W mainlines in the process, then again crossing the AC interlocking plant to head west onto the branch. Several of the Erie Lackawanna's cabooses were fitted with headlights and conductor air stands for use on the backing out operation of these trains.

The extremely slow reverse move often took thirty to forty-five minutes to complete, often hopelessly fouling both the interlocking plant and the vehicle traffic in town during the process. Just the opposite procedure was used for the return from Dayton, with the trains proceeding across the interlocking plant and on through the center of town, then backing through town and across the interlocking plant again to get into the yards. The complicated maneuvers involved in getting a train onto or off of the branch frequently caused a pileup of traffic on the C&O and the N&W, and it was not unusual to have as many as four trains of these two roads waiting to cross the interlocking plant just a few minutes after one of the EL Dayton trains cleared the plant. Since there were several streets which crossed the tracks of all three railroads this further fouled up vehicle traffic which had stacked up waiting for the Dayton train to clear.

The Mechanical Department controlled what type of power would be used on the Dayton Branch, and Charlie Dillon, the Master Mechanic of the Marion Shop, was a firm believer that locomotives operated best in model-matched consists. He also preferred to keep the railroad's oldest power on the branch lines, so that if breakdowns delayed a train it wouldn't be plugging up the mainline and obstructing higher priority traffic. The effect of his influence on motive power assignments was readily evident in Dayton Branch lashups, where the usual power was a trio or quartet of freight converted E8s, or a lashup of four F7s (frequently arranged in numerical order by road number). Occasionally a couple of extra "B" units would slip into the F7 lashups, or the consist of E8s might get as many as six units. Despite the fact that most of the locomotives in use on the Dayton Branch were approaching twenty-five years of age, the railroad managed to maintain them in good mechanical and electrical condition, and there were seldom any train delays due to the motive power.

The matched lashups of first generation power, the fairly restrictive track speeds allowed on the branch, and the close access by public roads made the line a favorite subject for local rail enthusiasts to chase. One long stretch of road parallel to the Dayton Branch just south of Green Camp, Ohio was a favorite spot for taking panned shots or just driving alongside the power and listening to the Model 567 prime movers of the first generation EMD E8 and F7 diesels lean into the tonnage.

The Marion Diesel Shops and much of the yard were built on low-lying land which could turn into a bog at some times of the year. The lack of support for the tracks contributed to derailments and damage to equipment, and as part of the re-organization following its bankruptcy, the Erie Lackawanna had planned o update and expand the facilities at Marion. The project would have included extensive track replacement and ballasting, and revisions in the layout of some parts of the facility. Some of the material needed for the rehabilitation project had been purchased and was on hand at Marion in 1976, but most of it was never installed, since Conrail chose not to purchase the westbound yard or the engine terminal, and instead retained only a small portion of the eastbound yard to serve local industries. The engine terminal and a portion of the westbound receiving yard were purchased by a railcar rebuilder as a service shop and storage area, while the tracks in the westbound departure yards were torn up and scrapped for their value. The EL had maintained a large sales and operating staff at Marion in addition to the Mechanical Department personnel who worked at the diesel shop. The 1976 inclusion of the Erie Lackawanna in the formation of Conrail and the resulting abandonment of facilities eliminated hundreds of jobs and resulted in the movement of many employees out of the area.

ERIE LACKAWANNA

Above: Erie Lackawanna GE U33C number 3313 and an SDP45 race westward past the tower at Griffith, Indiana in July 1972. The busy Griffith crossing and interlocking saw frequent traffic on the EL, the Elgin, Joliet & Eastern, the Grand Trunk Western, and the Chesapeake & Ohio.

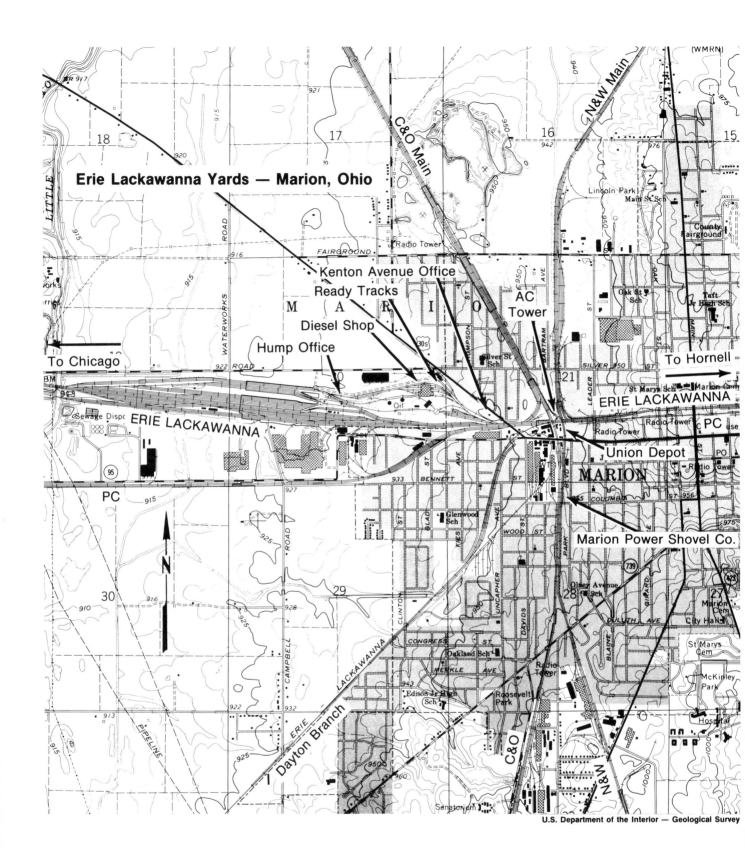

Erie Lackawanna Yards — Marion, Ohio

Kenton Avenue Office
Ready Tracks
Diesel Shop
Hump Office

To Chicago

ERIE LACKAWANNA

PC

AC Tower

To Hornell

ERIE LACKAWANNA

PC

Union Depot

MARION

Marion Power Shovel Co.

N

U.S. Department of the Interior — Geological Survey

Upper Right: With Erie Lackawanna GP35 number 2575 in the lead and an SDP45 trailing, an eastbound pounds across the EJ&E crossing at Griffith in November 1973. The EL GP35s, delivered in two orders built during 1964 and 1965, were likely to be seen on almost any type of train operated in freight service on the system. EL 2575, from the second order, also represents the second phase of carbody design applied to these attractive units.

Lower Right: Erie Lackawanna E8A 828, with a badly faded nose herald, leads an eastbound freight at Griffith in November 1973. By this time, there were relatively few locations left on the railroad which had full time crossing attendants.

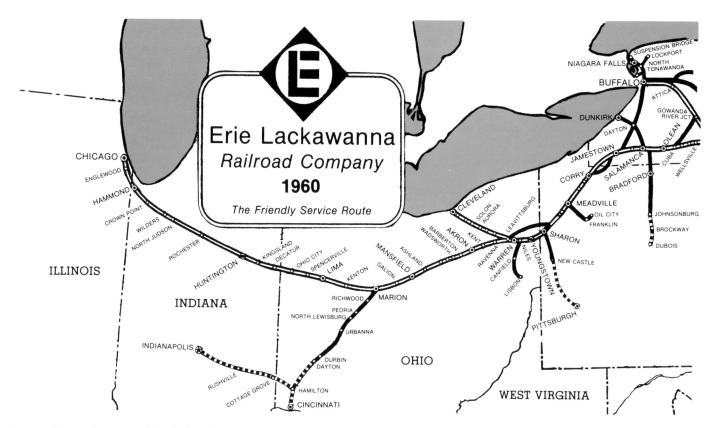

Below: The Alco model 244 diesel prime mover, used in the RS3 roadswitcher, was always a railfan favorite for its ability (due to turbocharger air delivery lag on acceleration) to produce spectacular displays of exhaust smoke. Even in such a routine operation as switching a short cut of cars, an RS3 could put on an animated performance. Erie Lackawanna E8A 832 and the assisting RS3 are shown making a setout in the Griffith yard in July 1972.

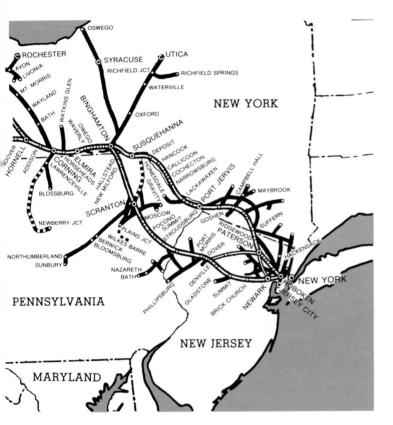

Below: The Alco RS3 roadswitchers maintained by the Marion Diesel Shop were used for yard switching and for powering locals, as well as occasional mainline service, in Ohio, Indiana, and Illinois. Erie Lackawanna 1019 rumbles past the depot at Kenton, Ohio in September 1972 with a local.

17

Above: Century 424 number 2410 is in the lead, with a Century 425 and a brand new Southern Pacific U-boat trailing, as this westbound freight races past barren fields near Lima, Ohio in March 1973. The Century 424s were maintained at the Youngstown, Ohio diesel shop and were seen on the "west end" less frequently than the Century 425s, which were maintained at Marion.

Right: There was only one bridge over the Erie Lackawanna mainline between Marion and Kenton, at Riley Road, and it was often a very good train watching location, as this May 1972 sequence demonstrates. A pair of SD45s had just headed west minutes before an eastbound with three E8As and U33C number 3306 rumbles under the bridge. Another headlight is just visible in the distance and a minute later Erie Lackawanna GP35 number 2560 roars west with a pair of new GE U30Cs destined for the Union Pacific at the rear of the consist. The UP engines were shipped from Erie, Pennsylvania to Marion, Ohio to be put into service, due to the favorable tax laws in the state of Ohio. Today, the bridge at Riley Road is gone, replaced by a dirt fill which spans a water-filled ditch that used to be the Erie Lackawanna right of way.

Above: Erie Lackawanna F7A 7124 (ex-Erie 712D), built by EMD in 1951, leads an F7B and a U25B westbound at the Prospect-Upper Sandusky Road gradecrossing, four miles west of Marion, in November 1973.

Upper Right: Minutes later, Erie Lackawanna F3A 7091 (ex-Erie 709A) leads a van train eastbound at the Prospect-Upper Sandusky Road gradecrossing.

Lower Right: The former Erie Railroad mainline was well known for its high overhead clearances, and the EL enjoyed a substantial business in high-wide traffic as a result. EL GP35 number 2571 powers a special move of two excess clearance loads in these coming and going shots taken at Marion in December 1973.

Overleaf: Erie Lackawanna E8A 817 was the only E-unit which retained its portholes into the mid-1970s. In this October 1972 scene, 817 faces off with an F7A at the fuel and sand facility at the Marion Diesel Shop.

ERIE LACKAWANNA RAILWAY COMPANY
EASTBOUND FREIGHT TRAIN SERVICE
TRAINS RUN DAILY EXCEPT AS NOTED
TIME SHOWN FOR INFORMATION — NO TIMETABLE AUTHORITY IS CONFERRED

Effective October 29th, 1972

CST		NYCB	2-NY-100	78	NE-74	TC-100	DM-98	PN-98	PB-100	NY-100	NY-98
Chicago	L		0430	0045	0945	1400		1800	2100	2230	2330
Hammond	L		0540	0300	1105	1530		1930	2205	2340	0100
Huntington	L		0850	0800	1405	1900		2315	0115	0245	0430
Huntington	L	0730	0910	0830	1415	1930		2345	0125	0300	0500
Lima	L			1115							
Dayton	L						E.S.T. 0130				
Marion	A	1030	1205	1245	1715	2330	0730	0300	0430	0605	0815

EST		NYCB	2-NY-100	62	78	NE-74	92	TC-100	RC-98	PN-98	CM-2	MF-74	PB-100	NY-100	NY-98
Marion	L	1155	1340	2100	2315	1915	0900	0130		1215		1500	0540	0715	0945
Akron "JO"	L	1505	1655	0230	0315	2225	1730	0600		1630		2100	0850	1030	1315
Kent	A			0305	0350		1800					2135			
Kent	L			0320	0400		1830					2145			
Cleveland 55th St.	L			0930							0001				
Brier Hill	L				0715		2130				0330				
Ferrona	L						2300								
Meadville	A	1755	2000			0115	0100	0930	L-Buffalo 0145	1930	0700	0045	1145	1330	1630
Meadville	L	1825	2020			0140		1230	1800	2045		0230	1215	1400	1715
Jamestown	L											0530			
Salamanca	A											0630			
Salamanca	L	2100	2310			0415	1530		2015	2345		0700	1500	1640	2015
Buffalo	A								0015			1015			

(RC-98 column: A-Rochester 0615)

EST		NYCB	2-NY-100	NE-74	NY-74	BS-2	BC-2	TC-100	DN-90	CB-2	BS-4	A/TC-100	PN-98	BA-100	SE-98	PB-100	NY-100	NY-98	TC-4
Buffalo	L					0930	1130	1715	1330		1930	2100							2230
River Jct.	L	2230	0050	0545		1245	1445	1800	1645		2300	2315	0125		1635	1820	2200		0145
Hornell	A	2315	0135	0630		1300	1500	1815	1655		2315	0035	0215		1720	1905	2245		0200
Hornell	L	2325	0145	0635		1500		2015	1800		0130	0400	0245		1730	1915	2330		
Gang Mills	L					1630							0430	0800		1830			
Elmira	L					1800							0600		2015				
Binghamton	A	0205				1800				2230	0415	0600		1100					
Binghamton	L	0215				1900					0445								
Scranton	A	0400				2100						0645	1000				2345		
Scranton	L	0410											1430		1300	1530	2355		
Slateford Jct.	L	0625											1830				0200		
Port Morris	L	0715											2030				0245		
Lake Jct.	A														1700				
Susquehanna	L	0245	0515	0945		1830			2030							2230	0545		0530
Port Jervis	A	0545	0815	1245		2115			2320								0140		0830
Port Jervis	L	0605	0825	1500		2230			2330	0515							0150		1030
Maybrook	A			1630					0130										
Suffern	A								0500	0700									
Croxton	A	0830	1100		2015	0145							2345			0415			1400

EST		BS-21	BS-51	BU-19
Binghamton	L	0130	0930	0045
Syracuse	A	0500	1230	
Utica	A			0430

92 Does Not Run From Marion on Sunday
RC98 Does Not Run From Buffalo Saturday
NYCB Does Not Run Mon. From Huntington
2-NY-100 Runs From Chicago Tues. thru Sat.
BS21 Does Not Run Saturday and Sunday
BU19 Does Not Run Saturday and Sunday

WESTBOUND FREIGHT TRAIN SERVICE
TRAINS RUN DAILY EXCEPT AS NOTED
TIME SHOWN FOR INFORMATION — NO TIMETABLE AUTHORITY IS CONFERRED

Effective October 29th, 1972

EST		TC-3	NY-97	NE-97	TC-1	TC-99	CS-9	ES-99	SC-99	ND-91	SLCB	NY-99	AB-91	PB-99	A-CX99	CX-99
Croxton	L		0315		1145	1130				2130	2200	2300			0300	0530
Maybrook	L			1015							0030	0130			0530	0805
Port Jervis	A		0600	1130	1615						0040	0140			0540	0815
Port Jervis	L	0430	0610	1430	1645						0340	0440			0840	1115
Susquehanna	BY	0730	0910	1730	1945											
Lake Jct.	L							1630								
Port Morris	L						1430	2030		2315	2350					
Scranton	A						1930			0200	0230					
Scranton	L								2330	0225	0240					
Binghamton	A	0800			2015						0415				0915	
Binghamton	L	0845			2115	0001			0115	0345	0400	0430	0130	0815	0945	
Elmira	L					0330							0445	0700		
Gang Mills	L	1245			0105	0445					0530	0630	0700			
Hornell	A	1415	1300	2100							0630	0750	0815	1115	1230	1430

		TC-3			TC-1	RM-97						ND-91		AB-91
Hornell	L	1445			0115							0635		0830
Rochester	L					1800								
Buffalo	A	1830			0430	2200						0930		1130

EST		MC-1	NY-97	NE-97	61	MC-3	95	BM-7	BM-9	TC-99	93	SC-99	SLCB	NY-99	PB-99	A-CX99	WCE	CX-99
Hornell	L		1330	2115						0500		0600	0705	0800	1125	1240		1440
River Jct.	L		1415	2200						0550		0645	0750	0845	1210	1325		1525
Buffalo	L							0030	1230									
Salamanca	BY		1615	2330				0530	1745	0730		0830	0930	1015	1345	1500		1700
Jamestown	L			0030				0715	1930									
Meadville	A		1900	0215				0930	2230		1030	1130	1201	1300	1630	1800		2000
Meadville	L	2000	2115	0345		2030	2200			0600	2345	1100	1230	1330	1815	1830	1700	2040
Ferrona	L					2330				0900		1500						
Brier Hill	L					0130				1100								
Cleveland - 55th St.	L	0015			2100													
Kent	A				0200	0255	0315	0400	1430			1645						
Kent	L				0215	0305	0325	0415	1440			1700						
Akron "JO"	L		0015	0645	0300	0345	0400	0445	1515		1400	1730	1510	1620	2115	2130	2000	2340
Creston	L				0530	0615			1900				1825	1945	0015	0030	2315	0315
Marion	A		0415	1045	0845	0845	0915	1115	2300		1000	2200						

CST		NE-97	MD-97	SLCB	NY-99	PB-99	A-CX99	WCE	CX-99
Marion	L	1045	1915	1750	1930	0001	2345	2340	0225
Dayton	A		2245						
Lima	L		E.S.T.						
Huntington	A	1400		2100	2230	0305	0250	0300	0525
Huntington	L	1410			2240	0315	0300		0535
Hammond	A	1730			0200	0715	0625		0840
Chicago	A	1930			0330	0330	0745		1000

EST		SB-24	SB-50	UB-22
Utica	L			2045
Syracuse	L	1900	0415	0030
Binghamton	A	2245	0730	

NY-99 Runs Daily Except Sunday From Croxton
CX-99 Runs From Croxton Daily Except Sun. & Mon.
A-CX99 Runs From Croxton Tues., Wed. and Thurs.
RM97 Does Not Run on Saturday
93 Does Not Run on Sunday
SB24 Does Not Run Saturday and Sunday
UB22 Does Not Run Saturday and Sunday
SLCB Does Not Run Sunday From Croxton
ND-91 Does Not Run Sat. & Sun. From Croxton

Erie Lackawanna Employee Timetable #3, April 25, 1971

Above: Erie Lackawanna E8A 822 (ex-Erie 822) rides the Marion turntable in this May 1974 scene. The unit was one of two E8As which were fitted with late design Farr filter grilles with vertical slats. The other E-unit so equipped was EL 813 (ex-DL&W 813), which had the late design grilles only on the left side of the carbody.

THE LOAD TEST was the final checkout in assembling a lashup of diesels to go out on a train. With the brakes set, the reverser was thrown and the throttle advanced to check that all units in the lashup responded with speed changes and to be sure that they all actually loaded. Locomotives which may have been idling over a weekend could generate a spectacular smoke display during the operation. **Upper Right:** In this July 1973 photo, a seven unit set of F's with one E unit headed by F3A 7094 pours out an impressive smoke screen as the hostler peels back the throttle. **Lower Right:** Awakening sleeping E8As could generate an equally animated response, as this February 1973 shot demonstrates, but the Alco RS3s **Overleaf:** were truly deserving of accompaniment by an orchestra, playing the final movement of Tchaikovsky's 1812 Overture as they turned the sky black with smoke in a pyrotechnic display unequalled by any of the railroad's other locomotive models.

Left: While a pot of gold would have been preferable, an RS3 at the end of a rainbow was definitely worthy of a photograph. Erie Lackawanna 1016 enjoys a shower at the Marion wash rack in October 1972.

Above: The sand and fuel facility at the Marion Diesel Shop provided one-spot servicing for incoming units before they were routed to the shop for inspections or to the ready tracks for dispatching. This July 1974 scene features Erie Lackawanna 3322, one of twelve General Electric U36Cs (3316-3327) delivered to the railroad in December 1972. EL 2522 is a GE U25B delivered to the EL in 1965 as part of a fifteen unit (2513-2527) locomotive order.

MARION, OHIO

CHICAGO & ERIE
WESTERN DIST.— KENT
TERMINAL LAYOUT
MARION, OHIO.
VALUATION SECTION I-5
SCALE: 1 INCH = 100 FEET. ANI
OFFICE OF DIVISION ENGINE
MARION, OHIO.

ERIE LACKAWANNA HISTORICAL SOCIETY COLLECTION

29

Above: The Erie Lackawanna operated transfer runs to both the C&O and the N&W yards at Marion. The C&O yard was just "around the corner" from the EL yard office, and transfers didn't have to cross the diamonds at the AC interlocking, but a run to the N&W had to be routed across the interlocking plant and up into town. In early September 1974, RS3 number 1038 is cutting over from the N&W to the EL yard lead near AC tower with a string of coal loads trailing.

Upper Left: Erie Lackawanna E8A 817 will be the trailing unit of a quartet of E8As awaiting departure on a westbound freight to Chicago in this March 28, 1976 scene. The trio of Alco RS3s on the shop track, in the background, have probably been serviced and are awaiting the Sunday afternoon operation of the Ashland Turn.

Lower Left: The platform at the Marion Union Depot was fitted with both fuel and water hoses, which remained in use into the mid-1970s for servicing mainline trains without removing the power and taking it to the shop. In this August 1972 scene, the boiler water and the sanitary water tanks are being filled on a pair of E8As on a business train. Harold Stone, the assistant to the master mechanic at the Marion Diesel Shop, holds the water hose on the tapered fill fitting while trying to avoid being soaked.

Overleaf Top: Five E8As and an F7A back through the west yard throat at Marion in October 1972 as they work their way into the westbound departure yard to pick up their train. The railroad seldom operated this many E8As together in a power consist, as each until had two electrically-operated engine governors, and the drop in control voltage through the locomotives and the jumper cables could result in the E8As furthest back in the consist failing to respond to the throttle.

Overleaf Bottom: UH-OH! Southern Railway boxcar 23633 met its soggy end in the creek which passed under the west end of the Marion yard. An inbound Dayton train, backing into the yard, went too far and backed through a misaligned switch, causing the derailment. The boxcar was full of paper, which soaked up water, making a load which the wreck cranes could barely budge. The car was finally scrapped by being cut apart in place in the creek.

Left: The AC tower located at the Marion Union Depot was an outstanding location for train watching. During the early 1970s, there were frequently 100 or more moves across the interlocking in a 24 hour period. In this June 1972 photograph taken from the tower steps, Erie Lackawanna U33C number 3310 and an SDP45 on a westbound freight are about to cross the two track N&W (ex-PRR) mainline on the east side of the depot.

Right: You could follow the smoke trail to find an RS3 at work. The hump pusher and many of the flat switching jobs in the yards at Marion were operated by the elderly Alcos, to the delight of rail enthusiasts. Here one of the "tubs" works near the west end of the yard in March 1972.

Above: The Kenton Avenue grade crossing at the east end of the Marion yard had a full time crossing attendant guarding the busy Erie Lackawanna and Penn Central joint trackage. Both the inbound and the outbound power from trains headed east had to work through the yard throat enroute between the train and the shop. A lashup of E-units and F-units about to take out an eastbound train waits for switches to be thrown in this January 1974 scene.

Upper Left: The Erie Lackawanna's U33Cs were ordered when the road was under Dereco control, and had many features following the pattern of units built for parent Norfolk & Western, including dual control stands for bidirectional operation without the need to turn the locomotive. EL 3314 demonstrates why long-hood forward operation of a U33C was locally referred to as running "hammerhead", as it approaches AC tower in June 1973.

Lower Left: Erie Lackawanna 2408, an Alco Century 424 built in 1963, leads an SDP45 on an eastbound freight about to cross the two track C&O mainline at the AC interlocking plant in October 1972. The 15 unit Century 424 fleet (2401-2415) was the railroad's first new power order following the 1960 merger, and was delivered in the Erie Lackawanna's early black and yellow paint scheme.

Below: This power lashup at Kenton Avenue in Marion on March 27, 1976, gives a rare look at two of the Erie Lackawanna's units which were seldom photographed in the railroad's paint scheme. Trailing U25B number 2519 are EL U33Cs 3302 and 3301, which were returned to the railroad from the Delaware & Hudson, and repainted into their original EL paint scheme, shortly before the EL became a part of Conrail.

THE DAYTON TRAIN

Above: The business cars on the rear of an eastbound inspection train are being serviced as a westbound freight headed by Century 424 number 2452 crosses the AC interlocking plant in this April 1972 view. Near the signal bridge support, Charlie Dillon, the Master Mechanic of the Marion Diesel Shop, talks business with EL President Greg Maxwell and another gentleman.

Upper Right: The Dayton Train was always a highlight of a day spent trainwatching at Marion. The complex movements required to get the train backed out of the yard and through the AC interlocking plant usually tied up traffic in the town and delayed trains on the C&O and the N&W for half an hour or more. Erie Lackawanna E8A number 831 (ex-Erie 831) on the point of MD97 eases through the Marion Union Depot as it approaches the C&O diamonds and the Dayton Branch turnout in June 1973.

Lower Right: Heading out of Marion on the Dayton Branch, F7A 7111 and F7B 7113 (ex-Erie 711A & 711C respectively) ease across West Center Street in September 1973, preparing to correct any misaligned switches in the small yard which serviced the Marion Power Shovel company. There was just time to grab a cold beverage and a snack at the Carry-Out before pursuing MD97 down the branch.

Left: A trio of E8As led by Erie Lackawanna 818 cut across the Franklin Street (Ohio Route 37) gradecrossing in Richwood on train MD97 in June 1973. This is the same train shown on the dust jacket of ERIE LACKAWANNA MEMORIES. Today, there are no tracks through Richwood, but the town's railroad station, immediately behind me as I took this photograph, has been nicely preserved.

Upper Right: An A-B-B-A lashup of E8As and F7Bs on MD97 approaches the Ohio Route 739 gradecrossing between Marion and Green Camp in May 1973. The string of empty open-side auto racks are enroute to the automobile assembly plants around Dayton.

Lower Right: F7s and E8s on MD97 skirt a farmer's field just east of Green Camp in October 1973. The Dayton branch closely paralleled route 739 for much of the distance between Marion and Green Camp, and the late afternoon departure of the westbound Dayton trains from Marion provided an ideal sun angle for photography of the train over most of its trip.

Above: The terrain along the Dayton Branch was more varied than on the mainline west of Marion. Westbound MD97 with E8A 818 leading passes along an elevated section of the embankment near Kings Creek, Ohio in this June 1973 scene. The afternoon pursuit of the trio of E8As, in superb weather, yielded dozens of beautiful photographs as the train worked its way down the scenic branch line.

Upper Left: An A-B-B-B-A lashup of F7s on MD 97 approaches the station at North Lewisburg, Ohio in April 1973. This photograph provides a more complete view of the area where the dust-jacket photo was taken. The picturesque station was removed in the mid-1970s, and the branch itself was pulled up several years later. Today there is little evidence left at North Lewisburg to indicate that a railroad ever passed through town.

Lower Left: Erie Lackawanna F3A 7091 (ex-Erie 709A), a 1949 product of the Electro-Motive Division of GM, races west on MD 97 south of Green Camp, Ohio in April 1973. The Dayton branch paralleled Centerville-Green Camp Road, from which this photograph was taken, for several miles. The road provided a terrific location for taking run-along-side movies or doing panned shots with a still camera.

Below: An A-B-B-B-A lashup of F-units power MD97 westbound in this April 1973 view, taken across the barren fields from Benton Road in Union County, southwest of Peoria, Ohio.

Upper Left: Heading for Dayton, the caboose of MD97 has just cleared the grade crossing at Centerville, Ohio in mid April 1973. The crossbuck still identifies the line as being the Erie Railroad, although it is thirteen years after the merger.

Upper Right: On a weekend, the tracks in front of the Marion Diesel Shop would rapidly fill up with locomotives as the RS3s from the locals, the yard switching jobs and the outlying yards came into the shop for servicing. Eleven of the Alcos and a trio of E8As are evident in this June 1973 shot, taken from the upstairs window of the Marion Diesel Shop.

Lower Left: The shop force checks out the brake shoes on the rear truck of EL E8A number 812 outside the Marion Diesel Shop in April 1973. While the freight-converted E-units were not as versatile as a roadswitcher, the railroad got good service from the elderly units as power for trains on the branch lines and for secondary freights on the mainline. Their principal use was on the line west of Marion, and on the Dayton branch, where the grades were very slight.

Lower Right: The lake next to the fuel and sand facility at Marion was actually a settling pool, and the surface was mostly oil rather than water, but it made for some excellent reflection shots. An A-B-B-B-A lashup of F-units is headed to the yard to take a train west in late October 1973, while a row of F-units awaits servicing at the sand towers.

Above: There was a very short distance between the east end of the busy EL yard and the Marion Union Depot, and the abundance of rail traffic could generate impressive jam-ups on both the railroads which used the interlocking plant and the highways which crossed the tracks. A pair of RS3s, flat switching at the east end of the Marion yard, have everything tied up with an unusually long cut of cars which they have worked out nearly to the C&O crossing at the AC interlocking plant. On the furthest track, a westbound train is creeping into the yard on this fine April day in 1974.

Upper Left: Erie Lackawanna Century 425 number 2457 is all dressed up with no place to go on March 28, 1976, just two days before the EL became part of Conrail. The freshly overhauled and repainted C425 waits with three sisters at the Marion shop for transfer to its new owner, the British Columbia Railway. The Erie Lackawanna did not renew the lease on the twelve Century 425s (2451-2462) and they all ended up in Canada.

Lower Left: Nearly new Erie Lackawanna U36C number 3321, its paint still crisp and clean, leads a pair of U33Cs west out of Marion yard in February 1973. The fourth in the lashup, in an obviously unusual paint scheme, is one of the S. J. Groves & Sons Construction Co. U33Cs, which were used in the transportation of fill for the I-280 superhighway construction in New Jersey. The unit was on its way to its new owner, the Burlington Northern.

Above: The thirteen SD45-2s delivered to the Erie Lackawanna by EMD in December 1972 proved to be the railroad's last group of new locomotives. The brawny-looking 3600 horsepower units were extensively used in the railroad's expedited trailer van and UPS train schedules. They were specially modified with oversize 5000 gallon fuel tanks which allowed thru runs between New York and Chicago without refueling. EL 3672 leads 3679 west at AC tower in February 1973.

Upper Right: Erie Lackawanna RS3 1015 switches cars near the Marion shop in this November 1973 scene. The impressive exhaust cloud, characteristic of RS3s during acceleration, is a result of the air delivery from the turbocharger lagging behind as an increasing mass of fuel is injected into the cylinders. The display doesn't necessarily indicate that there is anything wrong with the locomotive or the railroad's maintenance of the unit.

Lower Right: A trio of SD45-2s totaling 10,800 horsepower accelerate train 2NY100 (the UPS train) away from the Kenton Avenue gradecrossing in November 1973. The 2NY100 train could usually maintain the schedule on the west end with only two units, but required three for the run through eastern Ohio, Pennsylvania, New York, and New Jersey. Scheduled out of Marion at 1:40 in the afternoon, the train would be in Croxton by 11:00 the following morning.

Above: A light snowfall has blanketed the ground around AC tower as an eastbound Erie Lackawanna freight approaches with SD45-2 3676 leading an SDP45 on a sunny morning in February 1974. The open auto racks trailing the power will become a rare sight in later years, due to the toll taken by vandals and lineside rock throwers.

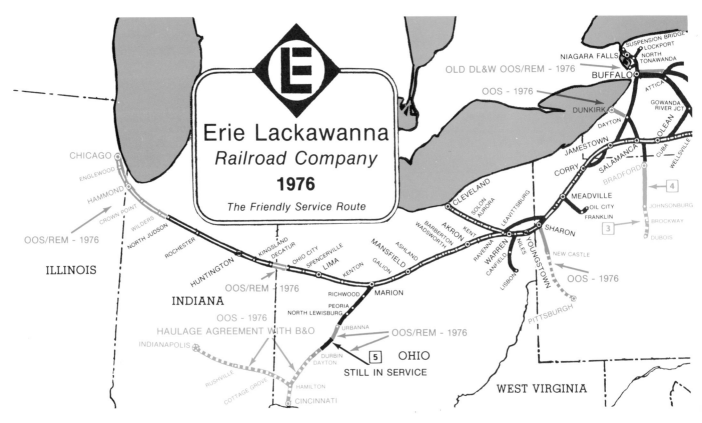

Above: You could frequently tell where a move across the AC interlocking plant was going just by the cut of cars trailing the engine. Erie Lackawanna RS3 number 1038 powers an interchange move for the N&W yard, working east across the plant in this March 1974 scene. The lead to the N&W was reached by a turnout near the extreme east end of the Marion Union Depot platforms.

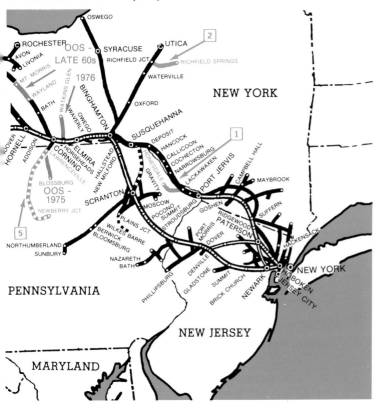

LEGEND

━━━ ERIE LACKAWANNA LINES

▪▪▪▪ EL TRACKAGE RIGHTS

━━━ OUT OF SERVICE

▬▬▬ NEW SHORT LINES OR
 ▪▪▪▪ OTHER RAILROAD USE

OOS - OUT OF SERVICE
REM - REMOVED

1 - LASB 1975
2 - CENTRAL of NEW YORK 1975
3 - P & S 1976
4 - CHESSIE SYSTEM 1976
5 - JOINT EL/NYC

Chapter 2   MIDNIGHT AT MARION

We never fully appreciated it at the time, but in the early 1970s, railroad enthusiasts enjoyed an extremely cordial relationship with many railroads, including the Erie Lackawanna. Those were delightfully innocent days, back before deluges of opportunistic lawsuits, extravagant damage awards by juries, and deceitful impersonations of railfans by the state and federal agents looking for regulation violations forced some railroads to view railfans as potential threats rather than interested friends and supporters.

The enthusiasts who took the time and effort to pursue photography of the Erie Lackawanna through the official permission channels found that the railroad truly was the "Friendly Service Route". The access and the benefits afforded to railfans who sought the railroad's assistance in the pursuit of their hobby were quite remarkable considering the more "closed" environment which had been almost universally adopted in the rail industry barely fifteen years later. In the 1970s, virtually every shop on the Erie Lackawanna Railway had photographic releases available for rail enthusiasts, which allowed the photographer to visit the facility and pursue his hobby on the railroad's property for a day (or longer by special permission). The railroad frequently arranged special visits for interested groups, and would even set up cab rides on freight trains on request.

The Marion yard was a twenty-four hour a day operation, and while the local interchange jobs around town tended to run during daylight hours, the through freights and the yard jobs were there to be seen and photographed throughout the night. Permission could be obtained to do night photography at the diesel shop, and the only restriction over daytime picture taking was a requirement to check in with the crew clerk at regular intervals. This was done so that he could advise the shop hostlers as to where the rail enthusiasts would likely be taking pictures, while keeping the visitors posted as to which tracks would see engine movements so they could keep in the clear.

The Marion Diesel Shop was equipped with tungsten spotlights in rows along the edge of the roof, which illuminated the ready tracks and service area effectively, though unevenly. There was adequate lighting to take open-shutter time exposures on most of the ready tracks, with exposures typically running between one and three minutes for ASA 25 film speed with a camera aperture of f5.6, and about half as much exposure time for ASA 64 film speed with the same aperture. Most of the night photography at Marion was done with Kodachrome II film (ASA 25), prior to the introduction of Kodachrome 25 and Kodachrome 64. Through experience gained in a number of night photography sessions at the diesel shop, it became evident that the effects of the tungsten illumination and the film color shift with long exposure times could be compensated to nearly a daylight color balance using a combination of an 80C blue photoflash filter and a CC10M magenta color correction filter sandwiched together. Once the desired color balance had been arrived at through the use of this home brewed filter, it was possible to take night shots in most areas of the terminal with no change of filtration and with only very minor modifications to the exposure time. The exposure and filter combinations were eventually used for hundreds of night shots at Marion.

In areas where available lighting was not adequate, or was noticably uneven, it was sometimes necessary to provide some additional illumination. This could be done either by positioning an automobile in the parking lot with its headlights shining on the area which needed light, or by hitting the "dark spots" with clear flashbulbs set off in a hand-held reflector during the time exposure. Using the automobile to supplement the shop lighting usually provided the best results, and eventually I added a portable 12 volt spotlight and a couple of tractor headlights to the night photography equipment, since they were often quicker and easier to aim than positioning an automobile to light the subject with its headlights.

During a time exposure, there is a natural tendency for the photographer to try to avoid any movement of lighted equipment or automobiles around the background of the scene, and to close the camera shutter prematurely if it became obvious that something was going to intrude into the picture. Usually the resulting photograph, with the exposure time only a portion of what it should have been, would come out only marginally acceptable. After a little experimenting, I eventually came to the conclusion that the movement of automobiles and locomotives in the background of scenes at the Marion Diesel Shop provided some interesting opportunities for dressing up night photographs, and it frequently proved possible to combine the light traces of ground lights and number boards of units on distant tracks as an accent in a photograph of units closer to the camera.

The engine terminal seemed strangely different after dark, and walking around the ready tracks at night was an unforgetable experience. The exhaust of the units usually hung close to the ground, swirling around between the diesels with the wind, and everything reeked of diesel fuel and smoke. The noise of the locomotives seemed amplified louder than in the daytime, and it was always startling to have the engine next to you WHOOSH as it unexpectedly blew down the accumulated moisture in the air reservoir with its automatic timer, or suddenly emit a loud THUNK-THUNK-THUNK-THUNK as the air compressor would cut in. The most animated locomotives of all were the Alco RS3 roadswitchers, which would alternately idle slower and slower until they would seem to nearly die, then gasp back to life with a resounding

CA-CHUNK-CA-CHUNK-CA-CHUNK and a plume of smoke as the diesel engine's governor would suddenly acknowledge the speed loss by jamming the fuel to the engine. The RS3s actually rolled from side to side as they went through their speed gyrations, and a night time exposure of an Alco would frequently show a sharp image at the rails which became increasingly fuzzy around the top of the hood and cab from the locomotive's movement.

The clear skies most favored in daytime photography were the least suitable for night photos, since the light tracks from the stars, smeared into long streaks by the earth's rotation, tended to compete with the subject of the photograph for the viewer's attention. Overcast skies were usually preferable at night, obscuring the stars and providing a neutral background which emphasized the subject. Foggy nights and rainy nights were superb, because low hanging clouds and wet ground could yield some of the best skies and reflections possible in night shots. A combination of fog and diesel exhaust hanging over the engine terminal could accentuate the headlight beams and exhaust plumes of the locomotives into brilliant displays, while the shop spotlights diffused into bright splotches suspended in the gloom of the night sky. The rain running down the side of the units formed a mirror surface which reflected the glare of the shop lights brightly, outlining cab windows, carbody doors, and handrails in far more detail than would ever be possible in daytime photography.

The night operations at Marion were a fascinating part of the Erie Lackawanna, but very few railroad enthusiasts bothered to take their cameras out at night and enjoy the show. For those who made the extra effort and ventured out, it was an experience they are not likely to forget. I spent many hours lugging cameras and tripods around in the dark, shielding lenses with an umbrella in the rain, trying to find dry footing in the quagmire of diesel fuel and water, and cleaning the crater grease leaked from the traction motor gear cases off my shoes at the end of an evening. The night photography sessions at Marion provided me with some of my most vivid and treasured memories of the Erie Lackawanna.

Above: The wash rack at the Marion fuel facility was constantly kept busy cleaning the locomotives which had been fueled and sanded. A quartet of freight-converted E8As is being handled by the rack on this April 1972 evening. Four or more of the streamlined units in a single lashup was unusual, and a symetrical arrangement was even more uncommon.

Upper Right: Demonstrating one of the photographic benefits of a location with an east-west track orientation, a westbound freight snakes into the Marion yard amid mainline tracks and yard leads brightly accented by the setting sun. The two tracks heading straight away on the left are the eastbound and westbound Penn Central main. The Dayton Branch crosses the mains in the foreground, in this October 1972 scene.

Lower Right: In the gathering gloom of twilight under a cloud streaked sky, Erie Lackawanna E8A 832 trails a lashup which will probably be on its way to Chicago by the morning. In this July, 1974 photo, the nose of the locomotive was accented by a single #2 flashbulb, fired in a hand held reflector during a time exposure.

Above: It seemed rather risky to be out taking pictures next to a camera on a metal tripod in the middle of a thunderstorm, but I reasoned that with all the locomotives and steel structures around the diesel shop and the service tracks, the chances of my equipment taking a lightning strike were probably minimal. On this night in June 1973, Erie Lackawanna E8A 812 has, curiously, just emerged from the wash rack as fog hangs over the diesel shop and thunder rumbles in the distance.

Right: Foggy nights yielded some of the best photography at the Marion Diesel Shop. On a Saturday evening in May 1973, three RS3s which will be part of the power for the Sunday turn to Ashland idle on the diesel shop ready track, starkly outlined in fog turned white by the glare of the spotlights. At the east end of the string, the headlight of 1031 cuts a brilliant path through the fog, while at the west end 1028 and 1020 are highlighted by the spotlights and partially reflected in a standing pool of water.

Overleaf: Erie Lackawanna RS3 1010 idles at the Marion hump yard office on a foggy evening in December 1973. The yard lights, the signal, and the locomotive's headlight etch luminous trails in the moist air, while a clerk handles the evening's paperwork in the office.

Above: This Dayton Train, backing into the Marion Yard on a foggy evening in January 1973, stopped momentarily to wait for switches to be thrown. It was just enough of a delay to allow time to set up the camera for a time exposure, and was one of the few times I used a telephoto lens (135mm) at night.

Upper Left: SDP45 3643 and RS3 1023 are almost fully reflected by a pool of standing water in this October 1972 scene at the Marion Diesel Shop. Locomotives moving through tracks in the background with classification lights and headlights illuminated left the accent streaks in the background, while the camera shutter was open for the time exposure photograph. The shop ready tracks were laid on soggy, low lying ground which drained poorly. After a heavy rain, the area around the locomotives was a good-sized pond.

Lower Left: The Erie Lackawanna SDP45s were truly distinctive. The units were built on the long SDP underframe to allow adequate space for a 5000 gallon fuel tank, rather than the 4000 gallon capacity of the standard SD45 model. The extended carbody had the rear end angled, rather than the flat end used in true passenger-equipped SDP45s, and the extra interior space was vacant. Erie Lackawanna 3646 occupies the diesel shop thru-service track, while SD45 3623 rests on the runaround track, in August 1972.

Below: The Erie Lackawanna's thirteen SD45-2 locomotives were delivered from EMD in December, 1972. The units were primarily used on the UPS trailer-van trains, but could also be found on expedited merchandise trains and in general freight service on most areas of the railroad. The 3680 is shown on the Marion ready tracks the evening of December 13, 1972. The locomotive had been delivered from EMD the previous afternoon, and was about to depart on its first revenue run.

Above: Photographs of F3 "B" units standing alone were hard to get, but a night shot of a fairly clean "B" was a real prize. Erie Lackawanna 6212, ex-DL&W 621B built by EMD in 1948, poses for a time exposure at Marion in August 1972.

Upper Left: Erie Lackawanna U33C 3306 idles on the Marion ready tracks in a May 1972 time exposure. The EL owned 15 of the General Electric U33C locomotives, three of which (3301, 3302, and 3303) were operated by the D&H for most of their careers in a swap for D&H SD45s 801, 802, and 803, which were run by the EL.

Lower Left: The Alco S2 switchers were active at Marion until late in 1973, when most of their switching chores were taken over by RS3s. After 1974, they were more commonly seen in service at Akron and on some of the branches. Nearly all the surviving units had been in storage for some time when the railroad became part of Conrail in 1976. Erie Lackawanna 507 idles outside the Marion Diesel Shop in this August, 1972 scene.

Above: The Erie Lackawanna inherited a large fleet of steel cupola cabooses from the Erie Railroad, all of which looked similar but actually consisted of several design variations with two lengths of wheelbase and partially riveted or all-welded construction. Erie Lackawanna C188 was illuminated by three #2 flashbulbs for this November 1973 twilight shot, taken near the Kenton Avenue yard office in Marion.

Chapter 3   **FROM MARION TO HORNELL**

The Marion Diesel Shops served as the maintenance base for locomotives used in a number of outlying locations in central Ohio east of Marion. The 1000 series Alco RS3s which were principally found on the west end of the railroad in the 1970s, were seldom operated on through trains, but were frequently used to service the automobile plants and switch the yards in Ontario, Mansfield, and Ashland. The need to bring them back to the Marion Diesel Shop for periodic inspections and maintenance led to the operation of pure consists of the elderly Alcos on the "Ashland Turn", a job which departed from Ashland on Saturday, working west for thirty miles through Mansfield and Ontario, picking up both freight cars and locomotives from the switching yards and industries along the route. The westbound turn would frequently end its last 35 mile segment from Mansfield into Marion by picking up interchange from the Chesapeake & Ohio connection near the AC Tower interlocking plant. The turn would usually arrive in the Marion Yard with as many as six Alco RS3s and several dozen cars. The necessary service and inspections on the locomotives would be performed by the shops on Saturday evening and Sunday morning. Any units found to have problems requiring further attention would be retained at the shops for work, with other RS3s being substituted for the Sunday run of the "turn". Late Sunday afternoon, the power consist of between four and six of the RS3s would depart from the diesel shops, pick up their

train in the yard, and head east to redistribute the locomotives and the cars among the automobile plants and switch yards in Ontario and Mansfield, with one or two units continuing on to the end of the run at Ashland.

Several other classes of Alco locomotives were found mainly in Ohio and western Pennsylvania during the 1970s. The railroad's few remaining Alco S2 and S4 switching locomotives (the roster had been greatly depleted by trade-ins on new locomotive orders) tended to congregate at Marion, Akron, and Meadville. Two of the most interesting examples in this class of Alco switchers were frequently seen at work in the Akron yard or on locals in the area. The Erie 520 remained in the black and yellow paint of its original owner right up to the inclusion of the Erie Lackawanna in Conrail in 1976, thanks to the efforts of local personnel who kept the locomotive's paint job touched up and hid it in the Akron engine house any time there was an official inspection train in the area. The locomotive became quite a local celebrity, and apparently either no Erie Lackawanna official with the authority to have the unit repainted saw it, or those who did see it had come from the Erie Railroad and didn't want to see the last example of the predecessor road's motive power repainted. Also based at Akron was the Erie Lackawanna 521, an Alco S2 switcher which had lost its original cab in a collision. A replacement cab from a retired Baldwin switcher had been grafted onto the unit so neatly that the alteration often totally escaped the notice of rail enthusiasts who watched the unit work.

The Briar Hill Diesel Shops at Youngstown, Ohio, maintained some of the Alco RS3 roadswitchers which were used in local switching and interchange work, as well as the Alco Century 424 roadswitchers that were used on heavy transfer runs to local interchanges, local jobs to the steel mills, and occasionally on iron ore trains. The Youngstown shop also serviced the EMD E8 passenger locomotive used to power the Youngstown to Cleveland commuter train, which was the only passenger operation on the Erie Lackawanna outside the states of New York and New Jersey after 1970.

The Erie Lackawanna maintained a small engine servicing facility at their yards in Cleveland. It was quite basic, intended for the sanding and fueling on the locomotives used in service to the ore docks, and in local interchange runs to the other railroads in the area. The Cleveland ore docks were the originating point for a heavy seasonal traffic in ore movements, which were usually handled by Alco Centurys based in Youngstown. Marion-maintained General Electric U33Cs which were sometimes temporarily borrowed from their usual assignments on mainline merchandise trains. When any heavy work was required on one of the locomotives operating in Cleveland, the unit was generally shipped to Youngstown.

Meadville, Pennsylvania, was the location of the major freight car repair shops on the Erie Lackawanna, which also serviced the caboose fleet and the road's maintenance of way equipment. Meadville had a small diesel shop which maintained a number of 900 class Alco RS3 roadswitchers, units which had been displaced from passenger service assignments on the east end of the railroad by the EMD E8s. (They in turn had later been bumped down by the demise of the long-distance passenger trains and the arrival of the General Electric U34CH commuter engines). The RS3s based at Meadville were used for yard switching and local work, while several Alco S4 switchers equipped with multiple unit connections were used as power on the Oil City branch due to weight restrictions on that line.

Working east from Meadville, the effects of the railroad's geographical assignment of their diesel locomotives could readily be seen. Alco switchers and roadswitchers, other than the Century 425s which were used in unrestricted mainline service, became much less common and the power in yards and on branches in the Southern Tier of New York state was more likely to be Electro-Motive "geeps" or switchers, units which were seldom seen on the west end of the railroad during the final years.

Between Cuba Junction and Hornell, freight traffic on the Erie Lackawanna mainline had two possible routings. The "passenger" main (which had the steepest grades), headed southeast from Cuba Junction to Wellsville, then east to Alfred and northeast up the river valley to Hornell. The line had fairly substantial grades between Alfred and Hornell, made more difficult by the frequent accumulations of leaves on the rails from the dense foliage and moisture from several streams which the line followed in its climb over the hills. Normally this line was the routing for the van trains, and expedited trains like NE74, which were assigned higher horsepower units.

The freight main, or "low grade" line, was a relatively straight run with minimal grades and fewer curves, and was the preferred routing for heavy tonnage trains with low horsepower locomotive lashups. It headed east from Cuba Junction, crossing a wide valley at Belfast, New York, on a high steel bridge, and intersected the "river line" just west of Swains, New York. The "river line", which connected Hornell with Buffalo, was a heavily used portion of the railroad in the 1970s, since it carried interchange traffic to and from westward connection with the N&W and the Canadian railroads. The principal facility serving the Erie Lackawanna in Buffalo during the period was Bison Yard, which had locomotive servicing facilities to support the switchers and road locomotives used in local industrial switching, transfer runs, and road service.

The "passenger" mainline from Cuba Junction and the "river line" from Buffalo intersected just west of the station in Hornell, New York, a town which was often best remembered by travelers for the fact that its two principal motels were both part of funeral homes. Located strategically near the geographic center of the Erie Lackawanna system, the town was the location of a major yard, a crew change point with crew lodging facilities, and the railroad's largest shop facilities, the Hornell Diesel Shops.

The Hornell Shops, managed in the 1970s by Master Mechanic Bill Collins and Shop General Foreman Kenny Gerbes, were the system backshop for the Erie Lackawanna diesels, handling all of the heavy overhaul work, the locomotive painting, and wreck rebuilding. The shop complex, which was basically a high bay steam-era central shop with its surrounding support building complex, had been updated for diesel work by the addition of several run-through tracks with elevated service platforms at one end of the high bay area. The shop high bay, equipped with heavy cranes which handled the Erie's largest steam locomotives in earlier years, was used as a staging and assembly area, and also housed the painting area and the truck shop. The portion of the shop which had been the machine shop in steam days served as the diesel engine build line for the Erie Lackawanna. Staging areas for building up diesel engines were spaced among the machine tools, and radial arm hoists and light overhead cranes positioned to handle the crankshafts, cylinder assemblies, and turbochargers for the diesels. The shop maintained a busy schedule of rebuilding the railroad's diesel locomotives, and was frequently packed with locomotives in various stages of overhaul, wreck repair, or painting. It also did the running repairs and scheduled maintenance for a number of road locomotives and switchers which were involved in the operations in central New York state.

When the Erie Lackawanna became part of Conrail in 1976, the yard and the crew facilities were retained in operation to serve traffic which remained on the former EL line. However, the shop complex was not retained by Conrail and changed ownership several times before becoming an electrical apparatus and locomotive service shop for General Electric.

THE ASHLAND TURN

Below: The ready tracks at the Marion Diesel Shop on a Sunday afternoon in April 1972 feature a lineup of RS3s which have been serviced and are waiting for departure on the Ashland Turn. The row of Alco S2 switchers on the left of the RS3s were mostly units which had been stored awaiting disposal to equipment dealers or scrap yards.

Above: On Saturday afternoon the inbound turn from the automobile plants around Mansfield, Ohio would collect the locomotives assigned as switchers at the local yards and bring them into Marion for servicing. In December 1973, seven Alco RS3s rumble past the servicing facility at the Marion Diesel Shop and are about to enter the westbound receiving yard. The Sunday turn to Ashland will redistribute them to their switching assignments.

Upper Right: The caboose of the eastbound Ashland Turn has cleared the yard and the RS3s have the train moving along smartly as they approach the Jefferson Street gradecrossing on the east side of Marion, Ohio. Once they clear Lincoln Avenue and Barnhart Street the engineer can throttle up and bring the turn up to track speed for the rest of the run to Harding.

Lower Right: Six Alco RS3s prepare to depart Caledonia, Ohio on a Saturday afternoon turn from the automobile plants around Mansfield. By June 1974 the turns to Ashland and Harding (near Mansfield) were one of the few jobs where RS3s would be found in road service. The distinctive "tubs" were generally being used in local jobs based in towns along the mainline, or on the branches.

Below: The Ashland Turn was always the main feature in a Sunday afternoon of trainwatching at AC tower in Marion. The cantankerous RS3s were by far the most animated locomotives on the roster, and frequently seemed supremely quarrelsome with having to work overtime on the weekend. The departure of the turn was usually marked by a cloud of smoke, incredible engine noise pierced by the ringing of engine shutdown alarms, and a trail of vital fluids leaked from elderly units. In this October 1973 scene, the eastbound Ashland Turn is approaching the C&O diamonds at the AC tower interlocking plant.

Above: Eastbound train PN98 is clear of Marion and the engineer has the throttle on the lead unit 817 "in the corner" as the quartet of E8As approaches the grade crossing at Pole Lane Road in April 1974. The ninety-six cylinders of the E-units' eight Electro-Motive 567B diesel engines pound out 9000 horsepower as the exhaust noise resonates across the open fields.

Upper Left: Erie Lackawanna 803, a former EMD SD45 demonstrator leased to the EL from the D&H, is on the point of a westbound leading a U33C at Martel, Ohio. The former New York Central line which crossed the EL at this location has been torn up, but the interlocking tower, which also controlled the access to the small yard and the leads to the local plant was still standing in October 1973.

Lower Left: Erie Lackawanna 2453, an Alco Century 425, and SDP45 3652 are westbound crossing the Penn Central mainline at Mansfield, Ohio in November 1974. This scene is a particularly graphic reminder of the changes which have taken place since the EL became part of Conrail in 1976. Since that time, both of the EL mainline tracks have been taken up, the Mansfield station has been torn down, the platforms removed, and some of the buildings in the background have disappeared. There is little evidence left at the location that the EL was there at all, except that the trees and brush are younger and shorter along the path of the old EL right of way.

MEADVILLE, PENNSYLVANIA

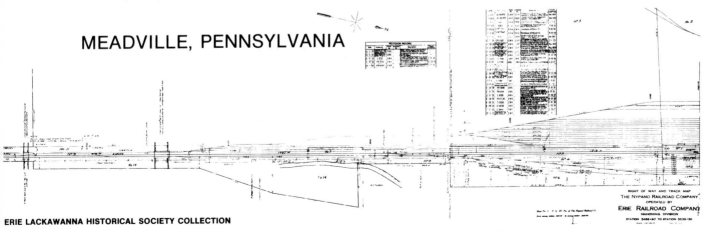

RIGHT OF WAY AND TRACK MAP
THE NYPANO RAILROAD COMPANY
OPERATED BY
ERIE RAILROAD COMPANY
MAHONING DIVISION
STATION 5488+60 TO STATION 5539+30

ERIE LACKAWANNA HISTORICAL SOCIETY COLLECTION

Above: Ontario Hill, just west of Mansfield, Ohio, is the last grade of any consequence that westbound trains on the EL had to contend with enroute to Marion and Chicago. In July 1973, SDP45 3662 leads U36C 3319 westbound at the summit of the hill, where Ohio route 314 passes under the EL mainline.

Upper Right: Akron, Ohio was home to two of the most interesting switching locomotives on the EL, resting together on the engine house tracks in September 1974. If something doesn't look quite right about EL 521, it could be that Baldwin switcher cab, which was transplanted onto the Alco after the unit was damaged in a yard accident. Erie Railroad S2 520 remained in its black and yellow paint scheme right up to Conrail, thanks to local employees who kept the old paint scheme clean and touched-up. The usual practice at Akron was to get the 520 into the shop any time there was an inspection train in the area, to prevent the unit from being seen by any officials who might have wanted it repainted into EL colors.

Lower Right: As the end drew near for the EL, most of the Alco switchers on the system were taken out of service and stored in the Marion, Ohio yards. In July 1976, a pair of EMD NW2s have taken over at the Akron engine house. A few years into the Conrail era, the yard would be closed as well.

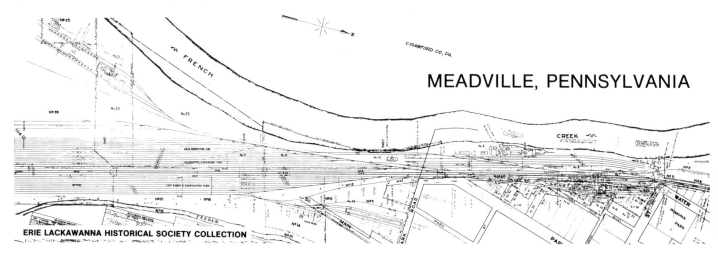

MEADVILLE, PENNSYLVANIA

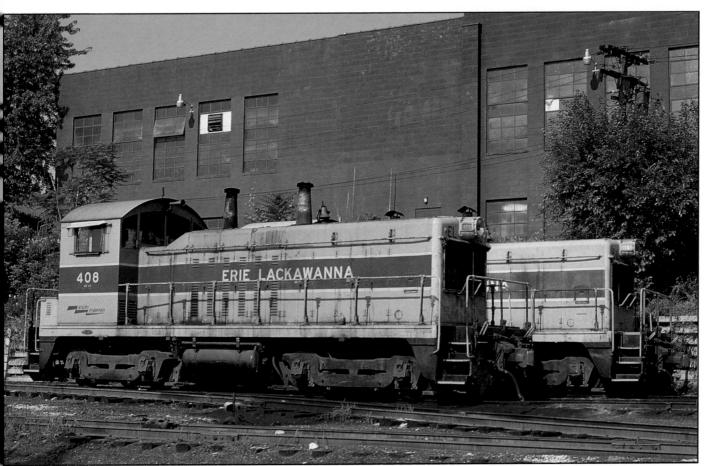

Above: Erie Lackawanna Alco S2 521, with its transplanted Baldwin cab, works the Akron yard in May 1974. The 86 foot auto parts boxcars in the New York Central, Pennsylvania, or Erie Lackawanna paint schemes shown here would become a rare sight only a few years later as Conrail initiated massive shop programs to eliminate predecessor roads paint schemes and reporting marks on their freight car fleet.

Left: Erie 520 works the Akron yard in October 1974 while EL 521, readily identifiable from a distance by its Baldwin cab, idles at the engine house.

Below: The large yard at Meadville, Pennsylvania, is the location of the EL's principal freight car and caboose repair facility. The yard was usually worked by 900 series Alco RS3s during the early 1970s. These passenger equipped units had been bumped from commuter service on the east end of the railroad and (by the 1970 delivery of U34CHs from GE) by the elimination of the railroads through passenger trains, which freed up E8As to take the RS3's place. EL 923 is working the yard in early May 1974.

Previous Page: The impressive bridge at Belfast, New York carried the low-grade line across a wide valley. The freight line which extended from Cuba Junction to River Junction (on the Buffalo line), was severed shortly after the EL was absorbed by Conrail, and the bridge was dynamited and scrapped. An SDP45 and a SD45 are the power on an eastbound train crossing the bridge in this September 1974 view. The nearly new 32000 and 33000 series Greenville and Bethlehem built hopper cars trailing the units were the most numerous single-design class of EL freight cars, and many were still in EL paint ten years after the railroad's demise.

Upper Left: A spectacular sky and dramatic lighting accentuate EL 2455, an Alco Century 425, as the unit heads a westbound train pulling past the station at Hornell, New York, in a September 1973 dark side scene. The locomotive was one of a group of twelve C425s built for the railroad in 1964, all of which ended up in Canada on the British Columbia Railway following the demise of the EL.

Above/Lower Left: Erie Lackawanna RS3 1057, shown outside the Hornell Shop at its completion in May 1973, was the railroads only Phase 3 RS3, the vertical stack of carbody filters in the hood denote this variation. The locomotive was assembled by the shop from the parts of three locomotives which had been in wrecks or had major mechanical or electrical failures. A Boston & Maine RS3 donated the distinctive hood, while other major components came from an EL RS3 and a Delaware & Hudson unit. The conglomeration was assembled by Hornell to produce the single servicable unit. In the fashion of a model railroad kitbashing project, the completed 1057 was spotted for pictures next to the pseudo-locomotive the shop had assembled from many of the leftover parts, which was on its way to scrap as trade-in credit toward a new locomotive order.

Overleaf: The Erie Lackawanna's main backshop at Hornell, New York, was a steam-era shop which had been modernized to handle both the running maintenance and the heavy repair of diesel locomotives. **Upper Left:** Run-through tracks had been installed in an addition to the building, and contained the elevated platforms needed for diesel locomotive servicing. **Lower Left:** Most of the high bay which was little modified from the steam era, was used to handle trucks, diesel engines, and major subassemblies, which were then rebuilt in other parts of the shop. On this day in April 1972 a pair of Alco Century 425s share the bay with a GP7. **Upper Right:** EL SW7 433 resting in the high bay with its hood and fan drive equipment removed, displays its 1200 horsepower EMD 567B prime mover. **Lower Right:** At the south end of the high bay, resting amid the Whiting hoists of the truck drop pit is partially repainted Alco RS3 1004, with its 12 cylinder 1600 horsepower 244 diesel prime mover clearly visible. The paint applied to the locomotive shows the EL's standard application sequence. First the entire carbody was painted yellow, which served as a finished coat in the exposed areas and as a primer in the areas which would be painted over with other colors. Once it had dried, the yellow was masked over, and tape lettering was applied, then the stripe was painted maroon. When the maroon had dried, it was also masked over, as shown on the 1004, and grey paint was applied to all the remaining portions of the carbody. When the masking was removed, the tape lettering would expose the yellow base paint. If the unit was to have a black roof line, as was done on many four and six axle roadswitchers, E8As, and F7s up until about 1973, the black paint was sprayed last, with roll paper draped down the side of the unit to protect the areas which had already been painted with grey, maroon, and yellow.

Above: Erie Lackawanna RS3 926 is being readied for load box testing in May 1974. At the completion of overhaul and repainting, the units were positioned outside and their main generator output was connected to an electrical load box, consisting of sets of resistance grids with a blower motor for cooling. This allowed the electrical system and the main generator to be checked out, up to the full rated output, without moving the locomotive.

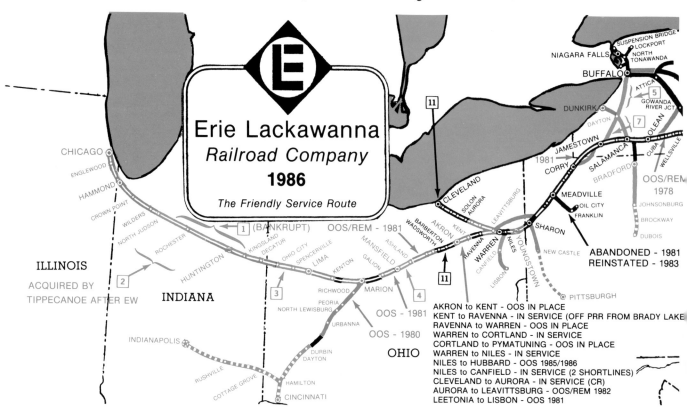

Above: The results of the Hornell Shop's time and effort are displayed in GP7 1244, shown complete except for the application of black paint to the rear truck.

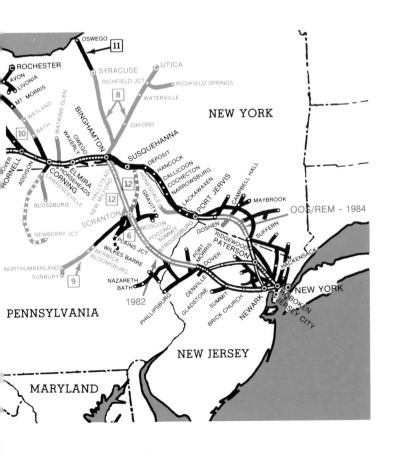

LEGEND

▬▬ ERIE LACKAWANNA LINES

▪▪▪▪ EL TRACKAGE RIGHTS

▬▬ OUT OF SERVICE

▬▬ NEW SHORT LINES OR
      OTHER RAILROAD USE

OOS - OUT OF SERVICE
REM - REMOVED

1 - ERIE WESTERN 1977
2 - TIPPECANOE 1979
3 - SPENCERVILLE & ELGIN
4 - ASHLAND RAILWAY 1986
5 - BUFFALO SOUTHERN
6 - STEAMTOWN USA
7 - NEW YORK & LAKE ERIE
8 - NYS & W 1983
9 - NORTHSHORE RR 1984
10 - BATH & HAMMONDSPORT
11 - CONRAIL
12 - DELAWARE & HUDSON

Chapter 4   **THE EAST END**

The Erie Lackawanna mainline east of Hornell, New York, ran through some of the finest scenery in the northeast. Just east of the Hornell yard limits, the Canisteo River valley narrows, with the railroad alternately running along a riprap shielded escarpment next to the river, or across farmers fields and through quaint small towns in the wider portions of the valley. At Carson, near the town of Adrian, the railroad literally had its "feet in the water", with the river on one side and high hills on the other, and during the spring and fall the early morning trains plunged through dense fog banks each time the curvature of the valley brought the tracks back next to the river. At the appropriately named Rattlesnake Curve, just east of Adrian, the railroad was again right up next to the river, sandwiched in with the parallel highway on a narrow ribbon of the valley floor, against a massive backdrop of nearly vertical rock cliffs. At some places in the valley, there wasn't enough room for both the road and the railroad along the foot of the cliffs, and west of Cameron, New York, the highway crosses the river to curve away up the side of a hill on the other side of the valley while the railroad follows the river through a sweeping semicircle, crossing the road again at the west end of the town.

East of Addison the valley widens, with the railroad gracefully following the gentle curvature of the Canisteo River. At Gang Mills, the Erie Lackawanna maintained a small yard and engine facility which serviced local industries, primarily handling sand and glass product movements from the glass factories around adjacent Corning, New York. East of Corning, the railroad followed the general path of the Chemung River through a wide valley to Waverly, New York, then paralleled the Susquehanna River east from Waverly to Binghamton, with the abandoned embankment of the former Delaware, Lackawanna & Western mainline running alongside for much of the distance.

While there was a connection at Waverly between the Erie Lackawanna mainline and the adjacent Lehigh Valley Railroad yards in Sayre, Pennsylvania, there was generally very little interchange traffic between the two railroads. The EL's main interchange partner in the Southern Tier of New York was the Delaware & Hudson, and that traffic was handled through Binghamton, where the EL motive power frequently shared space in the engine terminal and roundhouse at the D&H Bevier Street Yard with the Delaware & Hudson's equipment. The Bevier Street facility handled traffic flowing between the westward connection provided by the EL through Buffalo and Chicago, and the eastward connections provided by the Boston & Maine at Mechanicville and the Canadian railroads in northern New York state, Vermont, and Maine.

East Binghamton interlocking plant is the point where the former Erie Railroad mainline and the route of the Delaware, Lackawanna & Western divide. From ast Binghamton the former Erie line runs along the north bank of the Susquehanna River, following the river through Great Bend and into Susquehanna, where the railroad crosses to the south bank, climbing steadily as it approaches Lanesboro, Pennsylvania. At Lanesboro the line crosses Jefferson Junction, the connection with the Delaware & Hudson line from Nineveh, New York to Wilkes-Barre, Pennsylvania, then jumps across the valley on the beautiful stone Starrucca Viaduct. The line twists upward through Mountain Curve and reaches the top of the grade at Gulf Summit, before dropping into the Delaware River valley at Deposit, New York. For most of the years the Erie Lackawanna operated the line, until its downgrading in the mid-1970s, the former Erie main was a helper district between Susquehanna and Deposit, with the helper engines, usually F7s or GPs, laying over at Deposit.

Running east from Deposit, the Erie mainline followed the Delaware River valley, changing sides of the river several times in the process. Port Jervis, New York, marked the west end of the railroad's passenger commuter operations in the 1970s. The large yard at Port Jervis had supported the Erie Lackawanna's interchange operations with the New Haven Railroad through Maybrook, but once that business had evaporated with the inclusion of the New Haven in the Penn Central merger, the Port Jervis facility rapidly diminished in both size and importance. By the mid 1970s it was a sad and ghostly reminder of times past, an enormous yard with few freight cars and a large engine servicing facility with even fewer locomotives.

At Port Jervis, the Erie mainline leaves the Delaware River valley, ascending steep grades to the Otisville tunnel. At Howells Junction, the line divided into the passenger main, which ran through Middletown and Goshen (the line was removed by Conrail in the 1980s), and the Graham Line, which runs slightly further north through Campbell Hall. In the 1970s the passenger main saw several trains daily. The passenger main and the Graham line merge again at Newburgh Junction, and continue south to Suffern, New York, where many of the NJ Transit subsidized commuter trains terminated their runs out from Hoboken passenger terminal through the New Jersey suburbs. The commuter operation was home to the General Electric U34CH commuter locomotives and their push-pull trains, but the trains originating from Port Jervis in the morning and returning there in the afternoon generally used EMD E8s and GP7Ps with Stilwell coaches. The Suffern yard also serviced the neighboring Ford assembly plant at Mahwah, New Jersey. From Suffern the line continues southward through Ramsey, Waldwick, and Ho-Ho-kus on its way to the freight terminal at Croxton Yard and the passenger terminal at Hoboken.

The former Delaware, Lackawanna & Western mainline provided the railroad with a route parallel to the old Erie main from Binghamton to the New York metropolitan area. From East Binghamton, the DL&W main crosses to the south bank of the Susquehanna River, then passes through Conklin Yard, continuing southeast to Halstead, Pennsylvania, across the river from the Erie line at Great Bend. At this point the line leaves the Susquehanna River valley, climbing through several intersecting valleys which take it through New Milford, Pennsylvania, and the small towns of Alford, Kingsley, Hop Bottom, and Nicholson. The line east of Halstead was part of a massive relocation project in 1912-1915, and is one of the most impressive feats of railroad engineering in the northeast, winding along high up the sides of the mountains, barely visible from US Route 11 in the valley, which was built on the old alignment of the railroad. The line changes sides of the valley twice between Halstead and the top of the grade at Clark Summit, once between the towns of Kingsley and Hop Bottom on the massive Martin's Creek Viaduct, a structure which is longer and higher than the bridges on most other major railroads, but which seldom receives any mention because it is only a few miles from the railroad's second crossing of the valley, on the largest concrete bridge in the world, the Lackawanna's Tunkhannock Viaduct at Nicholson, Pennsylvania. Both words and photographs fail to adequately convey an accurate image of the Tunkhannock Viaduct - the incredibly massive concrete viaduct simply has to be seen to be believed.

From the Tunkhannock Viaduct the Lackawanna main continues east through Factoryville Tunnel and reaches the top of the grade at Clarks Summit, Pennsylvania. From there the line descends with steep grades and tight curvatures into Scranton, only to face another torturous ascent with steep ascending grades eastbound out of the city. The grades into and out of Scranton were one of the greatest operational problems for the Delaware, Lackawanna & Western and for the Erie Lackawanna. The DL&W, as part of the extensive line relocation projects of the 1912-1915 era, had considered a bold plan for a Scranton bypass line, which would have run northeast along the side of the mountains from Clarks Summit to Carbondale, where the line would have crossed the valley on a concrete viaduct nearly twice the size of Tunkhannock. The line would have then run to the south along the sides of the mountains on the eastern edge of the valley to rejoin the mainline at Moscow. Unfortunately the Lackawanna ran too short of funds to attempt the colossal undertaking, and the railroad and the successor Erie Lackawanna were left having to contend with the frequent need for helper engines on the grades out of Scranton.

Local business in Scranton, and traffic on the Bloomsburg line, which intersected the main at the west end of the yard were sufficient that the Erie Lackawanna was able to justify keeping the Scranton Diesel Shop in full operation into the 1970s. The Scranton shop, which had been the Lackawanna's principal diesel servicing facility, was a modern facility whose only real shortcoming was the fact that the interior service tracks had not been designed for the run through servicing of the locomotives. Consequently re-spotting the entire track was required if the unit furthest into the shop had to be moved. The shop maintained a fleet of EMD switching locomotives used in Scranton and the smaller yards in eastern Pennsylvania, and serviced the road power for the mainline trains and the operations on the "Bloom" branch.

The mainline east of Scranton reached the top of the grade at Pocono Summit, in the heart of the Pocono Mountains resort region. The vacation paradise provided little business for the Erie Lackawanna however, as the closely adjacent superhighways had drawn away the vacationers who once came by rail back in the DL&W era. After the Erie Lackawanna discontinued its through passenger trains there had been no further rail passenger service to the region, and the former DL&W line had become a freight railroad through some of the best scenery in the east. The line descended the east slope of the Poconos to Stroudsburg, where it followed the Delaware River southeast to Slateford Junction, the intersection of the "Old Line", which provided access to the Bangor Branch, and the Lackawanna "Cutoff" line, which had been built during the line relocation projects to provide a direct route from Port Morris to Slateford by crossing a series of valleys in northwest New Jersey on concrete bridges and high earth fills.

The Lackawanna Cutoff rejoined the "Old Line" at Port Morris, the site of a large yard and engine facility which had been downgraded to the point of abandonment by the early 1970s. The mainline runs east to Dover, New Jersey, the western limit of the electrified multiple-unit car commuter operations, and the location of a storage yard for MU and push-pull trains. Ten miles east of Dover, the non-electrified Boonton Line heads northeast from Denville Junction, providing a parallel route to the mainline which was frequently used by van trains and expedited merchandise trains to avoid commuter train congestion on the mainline in morning and evening hours. The electrified Gladstone branch connects with the mainline at Summit, where westbound commuter trains are split and eastbound trains are joined, to service both the branch and the mainline. The mainline continues east through

Orange and Newark enroute to the Croxton freight yard and the Hoboken Passenger Terminal. The railroad maintained an engine servicing facility at Croxton Yard to handle the switching locomotives used in the New Jersey metropolitan area and the road locomotives being turned around for the van and merchandise trains.

By the early 1970s the Erie Lackawanna's remaining Baldwin locomotives had been retired, and nearly all of the locomotives used on the east end of the system were either Electro-Motive or General Electric diesels, with the exception of the Alco Century 425s which were in unrestricted road service, and the Alco Century 424s which occasionally wandered in from their usual assignments in Ohio. During this period the Alco RS3s and the Alco switchers, which had operated in the area in the earlier years, became infrequent visitors on the east end.

The railroad's marine department operated from the Hoboken Terminal, and the Erie Lackawanna maintained a marine fleet to handle tug and carfloat interchange of cars with several connections on the New York side of the Hudson River. The five tugs operated by the railroad in the 1970s were the MARION, the HORNELL, the ELMIRA, the BINGHAMPTON, and the AKRON, all of which were designed by Joe Hack of the marine design firm of TAMS, Inc. The first two vessels had been built in the early 1950s by Jakobson Shipyard at Oyster Bay, Long Island, and the last three were built by the Bethlehem Steel Shipyards on Staten Island. All five vessels were sold to commercial service after the demise of the Erie Lackawanna in 1976.

Upper Right: Erie Lackawanna SD45 3623 leads U33C 3310 and an F7B about to depart Hornell, New York yard eastbound to head down the Canisteo River valley in June 1972. The yard served as a crew change point for mainline trains as well as a pickup and setout point for traffic from the line to Buffalo to be turned westward. The inclusion of a first generation diesel in the lashup usually imposed some traction motor amperage operating restrictions, but was common practice anyway.

Lower Right: A meeting at the east end of Hornell Yard in September 1973 has a pair of eastbound SDP45s facing SD45 3628, which is running "hammerhead" on the point of a westbound consist. The Erie Lackawanna's SD45s 3621-3634 and SDP45s 3635-3653 were financed by the N&W through Dereco, and were built to specifications similar to N&W units (except for having low short hoods) which included the installation of dual control stands for bidirectional lead unit operation.

Right: Erie Lackawanna SD45 3633 is on the point of a westbound freight in this April 1972 photo at Rattlesnake Curve. A pair of GP35s and an Alco Century 425 contribute their share to bring the consist up to a total of 11,000 horsepower, more than adequate to hold the schedule.

Left: The telegraph and signal lines are coated with dew and the morning fog still hangs heavy over the Canisteo River valley at Carson near Adrian, New York at 6 o'clock on an April day in 1972. The quiet of the valley is suddenly shattered by the approach of a westbound freight led by SDP45 3638. Emerging from the fog bank, the train thunders past the semaphore as it heads for Hornell, where a quick crew change will make it ready to resume its trip west to Chicago.

Left: The sun is about to set as Erie Lackawanna U33B 3308 and an SD45 race eastbound through Rattlesnake Curve near Adrian, New York, in April 1972 with PB100 in tow. This area of the railroad was one of the locations most heavily damaged by Hurricane Agnes.

Upper Right: An eastbound GP35-SDP45-GP35 lashup is reflected in the calm water of the Canisteo River as the noise of the diesels reverberates off the rock cliffs east of Rattlesnake Curve in September 1973.

Lower Right: Erie Lackawanna SD45 803, leads an Alco Century 424 and a GE U25B east near Cameron, New York, in June of 1972. The unit is one of three SD45s (801, 802, 803) which were owned by the D&H but operated by the EL. The "L" shaped windshield section, an unusual feature for a locomotive operated by an eastern railroad, originated with the units construction as an EMD demonstrator unit.

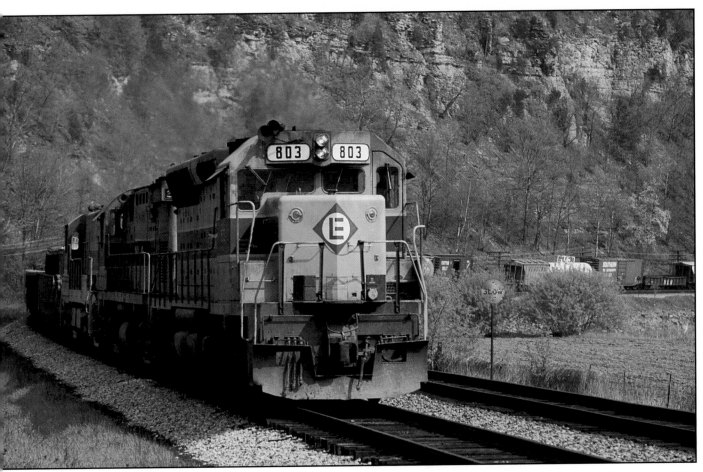

Above: This detour over the Lehigh Valley at Athens, Pennsylvania, in July 1974 resulted from a derailment which had blocked the mainline east of Waverly, New York. GE U33C 3305 leads an EMD SD45-2 on the eastbound train.

Upper Left: A pair of 2500 horsepower EMD GP35s, an unusually light lashup for a tonnage train, were westbound near Cameron, New York in July 1974. Normally there would be an additional unit, either a roadswitcher or an SD45 or U33C, in the consist.

Lower Left: Erie Lackawanna 3673, an SD45-3 delivered in December 1972, leads E8A 817 on an eastbound freight near Elmira, New York in October 1974. The 817 was the only "E" unit which still had portlights in the side panels after the rebuilding programs of the late 1960s and early 1970s.

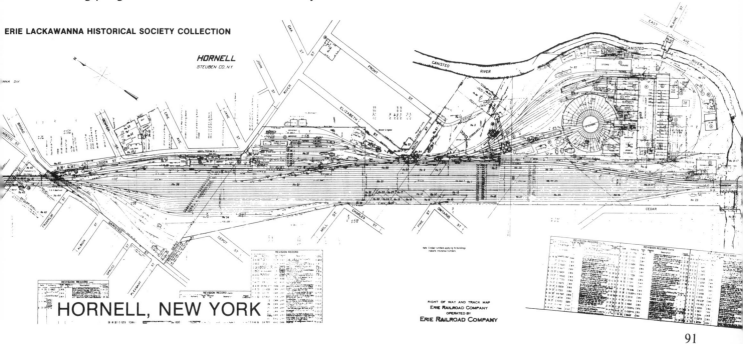

HORNELL, NEW YORK

Above: Erie Lackawanna 1409 is in the lead as a pair of GP7Ps head east near Corning, New York, in October 1973. The EL operated five "torpedo tube" geeps (1405-1409) which had been built with steam generators for passenger train use for the Lackawanna (as DL&W 966-970) in 1953. The roof mounted air tanks left more room under the frame for fuel and boiler water.

Upper Left: This caboose hop with SD45 3617 is headed west between Owego and Waverly, New York in October 1974. The lightly ballasted track behind the Erie Lackawanna's two track mainline is the Lehigh Valley line between Sayre, Pennsylvania and Owego, which passed under the EL east of Waverly, NY, and ran alongside most of the distance to Owego.

Lower Left: An ABBA lashup of F7s is in the process of doing a setout and pickup move from the yard at Gang Mills, New York, in May 1974. The yard services the industries around Corning, New York, and much of the traffic into and out of the area consists of the raw materials and the finished products of the large glass plants in the area.

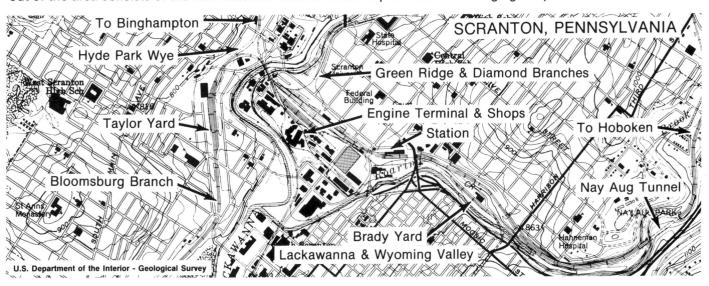

To Binghampton

Hyde Park Wye

SCRANTON, PENNSYLVANIA

State Hospital

West Scranton High Sch.

Green Ridge & Diamond Branches

Federal Building

Taylor Yard

Engine Terminal & Shops

Station

To Hoboken

Bloomsburg Branch

Nay Aug Tunnel

St Anns Monastery

NAY AUG PARK

Brady Yard

Lackawanna & Wyoming Valley

Hahnemann Hospital

U.S. Department of the Interior - Geological Survey

STARRUCCA VIADUCT

Built in 1847-48 by the Erie Railroad, it is the oldest stone railroad bridge in the State in use today. Viaduct is 1200 feet long, 110 feet high, and 30 feet wide at top.

PENNSYLVANIA HISTORICAL AND MUSEUM COMMISSION

Above: An F7A and a GP7P, the Deposit-based helpers on this April day in 1973, rumble across the classic Starrucca Viaduct on the former Erie mainline in Lanesboro, Pennsylvania. The units have just completed a westbound move and are heading back to Deposit, New York from Susquehanna, Pennsylvania, to pick up a westbound train which will be their next pushing assignment.

Above: Erie Lackawanna GP35 2569 leads sister unit 2582 off the Chenango River bridge just west of the station at Binghamton, New York in early April 1976. Both locomotives were built as part of a 24 unit (2563-2586) GP35 order which was delivered to the railroad in late 1965. The GP35s, which were maintained by the Marion shops, could be seen in freight service all over the Erie Lackawanna's system.

Right: The helpers move through the west end of the yard at Deposit, New York, on their way to Susquehanna to assist an eastbound train on the climb to Gulf Summit. Although based at the Deposit station for assisting westbound trains over Gulf Summit, the units would frequently lay in at the Susquehanna station between assignments if the next train expected to require their assistance was an eastbound.

Right: The "New Line" on the former DL&W side of the railroad between Clark Summit and Halstead, Pennsylvania, is a truly amazing engineering feat, with embankments cut high into the sides of mountains and massive viaducts to carry the tracks across the valleys. In this May 1974 view, a westbound train with a U33C-SD45-SDP45-SD45 power lashup skims along the side of the mountain at Foster Station, near Hop Bottom, Pennsylvania. The fireman probably has a good view of the cars the train is passing, hundreds of feet below on Pennsylvania Route 11.

Left In May 1974 a solitary Erie Lackawanna E8A bound for Port Jervis makes a station stop in Goshen, New York, with a three car train of the distinctive Stillwell coaches inherited from the Erie Railroad. The unusually large station sign reminds passengers of the fact that Goshen is the home of the "Hall of Fame of the Trotter". The passenger line across southeastern New York was removed in the mid-1980s, while the Graham Line, located slightly to the north and used primarily as a freight route was retained.

Left/Above: The early morning mist cleared just a few minutes before a pair of trains pass the stream and waterfalls just north of Tuxedo, New York in May 1974. A van train behind an SD45-2 and a GP35 is followed minutes later by the second morning train from Port Jervis, with the usual string of Stillwell coaches pulled by a single E8A. The short sighting distance and the noise of the rushing water masked the approach of trains at this location until they were literally right on top of you.

Right: A GE U34CH with a push-pull train is gaining on the pair of E8As on the point of a westbound Port Jervis train at the "S" curve on the former Erie four track mainline at Waldwick, New Jersey. The location has been a favorite with rail photographers in both the steam and diesel eras. It's a hot day in June 1974 and the lead E-unit is running with the nose door in the "air conditioner" position.

Upper Left: Erie Lackawanna 1403 at Scranton Diesel Shop, is one of the former Erie Railroad GP7Ps, which was delivered with a steam generator for passenger service, but without the roof mounted air tanks used on the former DL&W units. The GP7s and GP9s tended to congregate around the east end of the railroad, near the shops at Scranton, Hornell, and Croxton which maintained them, and were not often seen west of Meadville, Pennsylvania.

Lower Left: Like the GP7s and the GP9s, the EMD switchers were common on the east end of the railroad, but were seldom seen in Ohio or Indiana. A lineup of switchers on the ready track at the Scranton diesel shop in April 1976 features EL SW1200 458 (ex-DL&W 563), NW2 427 (ex-Erie 427), and SW9 449 (ex-DL&W 554).

Above/Below: The Delaware Water Gap, on the border of New Jersey and Pennsylvania, featured superb scenery and, during the Erie Lackawanna years, an ample supply of trains to photograph. Erie Lackawanna SDP45 3650, one of the 19 Dereco financed SDP45s (3635-3653) fitted with dual control stands, leads a GP35 and a SD45-2 eastbound through Slateford Junction onto the Lackawanna Cutoff in June 1974. Shortly afterward, a U25B hauling a converted steam locomotive tender and a Speno rail grinding train rumbles down the single track of the "Old Line", which leads through Columbia to Bangor, Pennsylvania.

Above: The former DL&W passenger terminal at Hoboken, New Jersey had served both the Erie Railroad and the Lackawanna since the consolidation of facilities in the 1950s' prior to the EL merger. The terminal continued to serve as the eastern terminus for the electric MU trains, the push-pull trains and the conventional powered Port Jervis trains during the EL era. In May 1974 an electric MU car train works its way through the track leads just outside the end of the platform canopy.

Upper Right: It is late in the evening commuter rush at Dover, New Jersey, and a train which has dropped off its passengers at the station is backing into the yard to clear the mainline. The large storage yard at Dover, with the interlocking plant controlled by a tower across the tracks and up a street from the station, was the originating and terminating point for most of the commuter trains on the ex-DL&W mainline. The use of any of the combines, like 3408 on this train, was a rare sight by May 1974.

Lower Right: The GE U34CH locomotives used in commuter service on both the former Erie and DL&W lines in the New York City area, were fitted with head end power equipment for lighting, heating, and air conditioning the push-pull trains. The units, operated by the Erie Lackawanna, were painted in a New Jersey Transportation color scheme to match the cars. In this May 1974 scene, 3365 crosses over from the yard lead to the eastbound main at the Dover, New Jersey station.

Above: Erie Lackawanna MU coaches and push-pull control cars line up at the head of the platform leads. Air hoses, steam pipes, and electrical lines between the tracks keep the car systems operating during layovers. The busy Hoboken Terminal handled tens of thousands of New York commuters daily.

Chapter 5 THE END OF THE LINE

The Erie Lackawanna ceased to be an operating railroad at 11:59 PM EST on March 31, 1976, but the sad process of dismantling some portions of the railroad and conveying other portions to new owners had begun weeks before the end, and continued on for many years afterward. Preliminary moves included a transfer of locomotives between the Erie Lackawanna and the Delaware & Hudson, to set straight some exchanges which had been made while the two roads were jointly operated under the control of the N&W owned Dereco holding company. The three former EMD SD45 demonstrators, 801, 802, and 803, which were actually owned by the D&H but had operated on the Erie Lackawanna for many years under the Dereco administration (since the D&H had no other EMD locomotives), were returned to the Delaware & Hudson. Two of the units ended up being repainted by their owner into a hybrid paint scheme which used D&H colors with the Erie Lackawanna styling arrangement. In return, the EL reclaimed U33Cs 3301, 3302, and 3303, which had operated on the D&H for many years to balance the SD45 exchange, giving the three units a complete repainting into the Erie Lackawanna scheme just days before the planned conveyance to Conrail. The Delaware & Hudson was also designated to receive some of the Erie Lackawanna's covered hoppers, gondolas, and cabooses to augment their own equipment roster for the expanded operations they would undertake as part of the trackage rights agree-

ments which accompanied the formation of Conrail. Most of this equipment was conveyed to the D&H just after Conrail began operations.

The Erie Lackawanna had elected not to renew the lease on the Alco Century 425 fleet, which had come due just before the inclusion of the railroad in Conrail, and as a result the lessor had negotiated a transfer of the units to the British Columbia Railway. The Century 425s were processed through the Marion Shop for departure from the property, and proceeded west during the week before the EL ceased operations, handling trains enroute. Several of the locomotives had been overhauled and repainted just weeks before the transfer.

Most of the Erie Lackawanna's equipment and facilities had been earmarked either for conveyance to Conrail or transfer to the Delaware & Hudson, but several of the shops were of no interest to Conrail and had been scheduled to close at the end of the final day of operation. The Marion Diesel Shop was one of these, and the shop employees had painted an enormous mural with scenes depicting the railroad, the shop, and themselves, along the inside wall of the bay containing the run through servicing tracks. All of them had painted their signatures along the mural. When I visited the shop the day before the end, the mood was one of somber pessimism, for the only certainty for the shop's employees was that none of them would be working at Marion any longer.

The next evening, a few minutes before the appointed time for the railroad to cease operations, Bob McCaffrey, the locally based General Electric representative, set up his camera and tripod to take a final photograph of the Erie Lackawanna. He selected EMD SD45 3628 and SD45-2 3671 as his subjects for a precisely timed night shot, closing the shutter at the exact instant the railroad ceased to exist. In Marion and everywhere else on the system, the Erie Lackawanna had become a part of history. Bob's shot of the two EMD's, the last photograph to be taken on the Erie Lackawanna, appeared as part of a commemorative article published later in 1976 in the Erie Lackawanna Historical Society's ERIE RAILFAN magazine.

In the months following the railroad's inclusion in Conrail, extensive relettering and renumbering programs were instituted to eliminate conflicting numbers and simplify equipment identification and reporting. Conrail began operation with over 5000 locomotives, 504 of which were conveyed by the Erie Lackawanna. The scope of the task dictated that temporary measures, however unattractive, would have to suffice until the system shops could get a handle on the repainting in conjunction with scheduled overhaul programs. The Erie Lackawanna's identity was slowly lost under a patchwork of hastily applied reletterings, usually done with a paint roller in whatever color might be available, and finished off with whatever stick-on numbers from Penn Central or the other Conrail component railroads were available for application.

The Erie Lackwanna had stored a number of locomotives, primarily Alco switchers, Alco RS3s, and EMD freight converted E8As at Marion and other locations on the system as a result of the general economic slowdown of 1975. Some of these units had major mechanical or electrical component failures which the railroad had not been able to repair due to its limited finances during the last few months of independent operation, and many were never repaired or operated by Conrail. Some of the units did receive Conrail renumberings, and several days after the Marion shops were closed the stored locomotives were moved to the Penn Central facility at Buckeye Yard in Columbus, Ohio. Within a few months, the older unservicable units began to be disposed of, and throughout 1977 and 1978 Erie Lackawanna locomotives were frequently seen being cut up at Pielet Brothers in McCook, Illinois (the scrap yard used by EMD), at Naporano Iron and Metals near Newark, New Jersey, at Striegel Railway Equipment in Baltimore, Maryland, and in the yards of other scrappers and railroad equipment dealers.

The freight cars which were conveyed to the Delaware & Hudson, had their reporting marks changed almost immediately to avoid confusion with Conrail's former Erie Lackawanna rolling stock. The EL freight car fleet underwent a much slower change than was the case with the locomotives. The rolling stock fleet conveyed to Conrail by the bankrupt predecessors was greatly in excess of the consolidated railroad's requirements, and groups of the oldest and least desirable cars headed for the scrap lines immediately or were retired after very short times in service with the new owner. The cars most quickly disposed of from the Erie Lackawanna rolling stock included the oldest classes of two-bay covered hoppers and most of the forty foot boxcars. The covered hoppers were usually scrapped on retirement, but the retired boxcars were suitable for a number of uses, and across the street from the Marion Diesel Shop a large boxcar field sprang up, operated by a local scrap dealer who offered them for sale to local farmers as storage sheds. Within a few years after the demise of the EL there were hundreds of the forty foot boxcars in the field, minus their trucks which had been either scrapped or salvaged.

The revenue rolling stock retained by Conrail gradually went through repair and repaint programs, and the frequency with which the Erie Lackawanna's diamond herald would be seen in the cars of a Conrail freight train diminished rapidly. A survey of the freight cars which remained in Erie Lackawanna paint scheme and reporting marks, taken ten years into Conrail, disclosed that the covered hoppers, the flat cars, and the box cars which remained painted EL were very few in number. At the same time, the largest remaining groups of Erie Lackawanna cars still painted and lettered for the railroad were a small percentage of the various classes of gondolas and about fifteen percent of the original group of 32000 and 33000 series hopper cars, the gons and hoppers being car types which normally require little running maintenance and infrequent repainting.

And so, gradually, the end came to the Erie Lackawanna. The locomotives and the rolling stock melted away under the heat of cutting torches, or had their identity changed by hastily applied paint and adhesive backed numbers, while the sections of the railroad not conveyed to Conrail or rescued by new owners were gradually torn up for salvage or slowly deteriorated as nature reclaimed the right-of-way. Some of the Erie Lackawanna's employees went to other jobs in different cities, working for Conrail. Others left the area the EL had served to seek employment with other railroads elsewhere in the country. Many, however, left the railroad industry altogether. Ten years after the end came for the Erie Lackawanna, there were still a few reminders that the railroad had existed, but they were getting to be few and far between.

Above: The Erie Lackawanna painted two locomotives and a caboose in a red, white, and blue scheme to celebrate the Bicentennial year of 1976. Unfortunately the railroad did not survive long enough to participate further in the celebration of the July 4th anniversary. Erie Lackawanna SD45 3632 and SDP45 3638 are shown at the IHB Riverdale Yard, in Illinois, on April, 1976.
Photo by: Paul Hunnell

Below: The three 800 series SD45s (former EMD demonstrators) which were owned by the Delaware & Hudson, but operated by the EL, were returned to their owner prior to the inclusion of the EL in Conrail. D&H 803, shown in a paint scheme which incorporates a blue stripe and D&H heralds in what is otherwise still an Erie Lackawanna paint scheme, is shown at the D&H Colonie Shops in July 1976. The unit was later sold for use in Mexico.

Above: The slowdown of the economy and the Erie Lackawanna's shortage of operating funds in 1975 and early 1976 resulted in many units with electrical or mechanical problems being sidetracked for lack of money to make repairs. By the end of March, 1976, the Marion dead line stretched for most of the length of the yard. Following the EL's inclusion in Conrail, many of the dead units were moved to the former Penn Central Buckeye Yard in Columbus, Ohio. Most of them never ran again, and ended up in scrap yards by the following year.

Upper Right: Many of the older diesel locomotives inherited by Conrail from predecessor railroads were already being scrapped only a year or two after the formation of the new railroad. A view of Pielet Brothers Scrap yard in McCook, Illinois, taken from the Joliet Road bridge on June 1977, shows an assortment of EL and PC Alco switchers and EMD F units awaiting scrapping. The distinctive Baldwin cab which had been installed on the EL Alco S2 521 following wreck damage prominently identifies that unit in the scrap line of Alco switchers in the background.

Lower Right: The formation of Conrail resulted in the disposal of many older freight cars from the predecessor lines. A large boxcar field sprang up in the scrap yard across the street from the Marion Diesel Shop, and in the late 1970s as many as a hundred of the former EL forty foot boxcars could be seen in various stages of scrapping. Many of the cars, removed from their trucks, were sold to local farmers as storage sheds.

Below: Conrail's initial motive power fleet passed along from the predecessor railroads numbered more than 4000 units, and presented a massive repainting and relettering project. Until the railroad was able to catch up with the situation through complete repaints and overhauls, temporary identity changes, however unattractive, had to be sufficient. Conrail SDP45 6673 (former EL 3641) shows the results of temporary relettering and renumbering, using Penn Central numbers, at 59th street enginehouse in Chicago, in October 1977.

Chapter 6 THE ELECTRIC ENCORE

As the locomotives, rolling stock, and mainlines of what had been the Erie Lackawanna railroad were being scrapped or altered by new owners, one of the railroad's most interesting operations continued almost unaltered for nearly eight years after the departure of the EL. The electric MU car operations on several lines in New Jersey, which the EL had inherited from the DL&W, had been in operation since January 21, 1931. The venerable powered coaches and unpowered trailers, variously called "grinders" and "wickerliners" by commuters, had seen few alterations in more than fifty years of continuous service. Even the merger which created the Erie Lackawanna had little visual impact on the MU car fleet - just the addition of "ERIE" on the letterboard of each car, neatly offset so that the existing "LACKAWANNA" lettering didn't have to be repainted.

The electrified territory of the former DL&W lines extends west from the Hoboken Passenger Terminal through Newark and Orange to Summit, where westbound trains are split into two sections, one for the mainline and one for the Gladstone Branch. From Summit the mainline continues west through Denville to the end of the electrified territory at Dover, while the Gladstone Branch runs southwest through Bernardsville and Peapack to a small storage yard at the end of the branch in Gladstone. This branch is an unusually scenic line, with quaint small towns, attractive old stations, and even a high trestle, and was always a

favorite subject of rail photographers who followed the operations of the MU cars.

The 3000 volt direct-current power distribution system represented the latest technology when cars were put into operation in the 1930s, but over the years the system had been rendered obsolete by the development of more efficient alternating current systems which could use readily available 60 cycle commercially generated power. Replacement of the Erie Lackawanna's fleet of MU cars had been in the initial stages even before the EL disappeared into Conrail, but the long lead time necessary to convert the catenary on the former DL&W system to a configuration suitable for AC power transmission kept the old cars running. Installation of updated signal systems and track improvements pushed the implementation of the project back until nearly eight years after the EL ceased to exist.

During this delay period the MU car fleet, operated by NJ Transit, provided the only opportunity to see a concentration of equipment in regular service which was largely unaltered in appearance from its days under control of the Erie Lackawanna. Although NJ Transit experimented with three modified paint schemes using red, red-orange, and orange (each with buff window strakes), only a fraction of the MU car fleet received one of the modified paint schemes before a switch was made back to the original green paint. Throughout the 1976-1984 period of the electric ncore, the majority of the cars in the equipment fleet remained in Erie Lackawanna lettering and the green paint scheme they had worn for most of their operating life.

While the electric MU car operations had long been a favorite subject of local railroad enthusiasts, it took some time after the demise of the Erie Lackawanna for the operation to achieve widespread attention. As the Erie Lackawanna diesel locomotive fleet and rolling stock slowly lost its identity to the scrappers torch or the paint schemes of new owners, the audience of train watchers at trackside in the electrified territory gradually increased. During the final months of the MU cars operation, it became difficult to take a photograph at some of the more popular trackside locations during the morning and evening rush hours without getting another photographer in the picture.

In 1980, I had relocated from the midwest back to the east coast, living in New Jersey only a short distance from the electrified lines. It was both a sad reunion with the last remains of a railroad which had failed, and a last chance to mount a campaign to photograph once more some favorite subjects which had only a limited time left to operate. During the 1970s, when I was living in Ohio, my opportunities to photograph the electrics had been limited by the substantial travel distance to New Jersey, and I had never been able to give the MU cars the attention the subject deserved. Despite delays in the rebuilding of the catenary and the installation of improved signaling systems, it was evident after 1980 that the multiple unit cars had little time left in operation. From 1980 through the end of the MU cars operation in 1984, I photographed the cars whenever the opportunity presented itself, concentrating on the almost unlimited night photography possibilities posed by the quaint yard and station at Gladstone, New Jersey.

Night photography at Gladstone presented significantly greater challenges than my earlier efforts at Marion, where the large tungsten spotlights on the shop had provided most of the illumination for night shots, and it was only necessary to fill in shadows with a few flashbulbs. At Gladstone, the only available lighting was from a few incandescent bulbs on the station and a row of mercury vapor lights along the street. Large areas of the yard were in partial to total shadow, but the offensive blue-green glare of the mercury vapor lights managed to discolor most of the background while providing very little useful illumination for setting up cameras and equipment. My first test shots at the yard confirmed that there would have to be a way to eliminate the mercury vapor lights from the photograph, in order to get rid of the blue-green tint, and then most of the illumination would have to be provided by flashbulbs, to allow control of both the angle and the color balance of the illumination.

In previous night photographs where I had to work around mercury vapor lighting, I had frequently employed the technique of "blasting out" the lights by hitting their photoelectric control cell with a direct shot from a bright flashbulb at close range. This shuts the mercury vapor light off immediately, and also tends to blind the photoelectric cell for a few minutes. The mercury vapor light has to go through its relighting cycle, which also takes a minute or two, so the photographer generally gets about two minutes to set off his flashbulbs on the subject while the mercury vapor light is shut down.

Unfortunately, the lights at Gladstone were installed in a row about a hundred feet apart, and by the time they all could be shut off sequentially by this technique, the first light in the row would be about ready to light up again. Shutting off the entire group of lights in the parking lot would not have worked either, since it would have plunged the entire area into total darkness, eliminating all the light for setting up equipment or walking around the station. The eventual solution, which was used in all the night shots in this chapter, was to mask the lights with partial covers which were hoisted into place with long poles. This eliminated the offensive lighting from the rows of MU cars in the yard while maintaining the illumination of the parking lot and station platforms.

The bulb to subject distances at Gladstone tended to be more than fifty feet, and for working with ASA 64 Kodachrome film it was necessary to use the massive Sylvania #3 photoflash bulb (a product they no longer manufacture), which was nicknamed the "Tactical Thermo-nuclear Flashbulb". This combination of flashbulb and film would typically allow working with a camera aperture of f5.6, which was adequate to keep subjects in focus from about twenty feet out to infinity. To keep the useful bulb lighting at a maximum, as well as to accentuate warm tones, I usually used clear flashbulbs, which provided the additional benefit of lightening the green color of the MU cars to some extent. When it was possible to use closer bulb to subject distances, by setting off bulbs from behind train cars on adjacent tracks, or by using the station or the catenary supports as a shield, I conserved the #3 bulbs by substituting smaller, and more readily available, Sylvania #2 bulbs, with no change in aperture.

The photographic technique used at Gladstone was open-shutter flash or "color painting". In this method, the aperture is stopped down to the desired setting and the camera shutter is opened, then the photographer walks along the subject at a more or less uniform bulb to subject distance and sets off the flashbulbs one at a time in a hand held reflector, then walks back to the camera to close the shutter. The film sees the flashes individually, but overlaps their exposure to produce a fairly uniform overall illumination. Since the entire effective burn of the flashbulb is used, rather than just a small portion of the middle of the burn captured by the action of the camera shutter, the effective illumination from the flashbulbs is much greater than that achieved in conventional flash photography. Also, because there is a degree of reciprocity involved in the exposure of the film (ie: the effective film speed slows down with increased exposure time), areas of the scene that have already been lighted tend to be less sensitive to additional lighting from subsequent flashes. This makes it possible to evenly and effectively overlap the illumination, and also makes it possible to use some already-lighted parts of the scene as a "blind" for setting off flashbulbs to light other areas of the photograph. This light blinding technique is evident in some of the photographs in this chapter, where it is obvious that I was in the scene to set off a flashbulb due to the bulb lighting trace on the ground, but there is no image of me in the picture.

Having complete control of the illumination of the subject provides the photographer with an almost unlimited range of possibilities for handling the execution of a photograph. Large areas of the scene can be masked out by avoiding lighting them, or by "dodging" the light through use of standing equipment, buildings, or cardboard sheets as light masks. The background at the Gladstone Yard was selectively illuminated by setting off flashbulbs from behind the standing rows of MU cars, and mud puddles were turned into "Scenic Lake Gladstone" by mounting the camera upside down on the tripod with its viewing prism almost in the water (aimed and focused by use of a right angle viewing adaptor) and relying on the intense flash illumina-

tion to generate a perfect reflected image.

Some of the night shot projects at Gladstone required more than a dozen flashbulbs, and the choreography of opening camera shutters, setting off a dozen or more bulbs, and then fumbling back to the cameras in the dark (while partially blinded by the effect of the flashbulbs) would have strained the ability of a photographer working alone. I was fortunate in having a group of experienced railroad photographers living in the general area who I could call on for assistance when a large project was to be undertaken. While I have long ago lost track of who was present on what night for which photographs, I would like to acknowledge the assistance which was provided by Charles P. ("Sandy") Burton, Jim Boyd, and Larry DeYoung, all of whom assisted in the operation of the cameras or the flashbulb illumination for some of the photographs which were taken during this project.

It should be noted that the night shots in the Gladstone Yard were undertaken with a great respect for the potential hazards present in a railroad yard at night. All of the night photographs in this chapter were done on Sunday evenings after the last train had arrived, when there was to be no further movement of equipment around the yard until the first train departed on Monday morning. Railroads are a potentially dangerous place, day or night, and proper official permission should always be obtained for photography on railroad property, regardless of what time of day. All photographs of the Erie Lackawanna Railway in this book were done with the official permission and approval of the railroad, either through the issuance of individual photographic releases or under the auspices of a railroad issued system-wide pass.

Upper Right: Two variations of the NJ transit paint scheme applied to the ex-Erie Lackawanna MU cars are evident in this photograph taken at South Orange, New Jersey during the last weeks of operation of the cars in August, 1984. The red or orange cars with buff window strakes, dubbed "Toonerville Trolleys" by unimpressed railfans, were a short-lived experiment. The final series of repaintings of the elderly cars were done in the traditional green paint.

Lower Right: An eastbound MU train eases through Gladstone headed for Peapack and Hoboken in November 1980. Other than the fading of the paint, there are few visible signs that the operator is NJ transit rather than the Erie Lackawanna.

Above: In one of the nation's densely populated states, there is still plenty of open country running along the Gladstone Branch west of Bernardsville. In this November 1980 view, a late morning train heads west from Bernardsville to make its turn-around at Gladstone. Wooden catenary poles and the rural setting convey a feeling of remoteness, when in fact the crowded New York metropolitian area is only a short train ride away.

Upper Right: A pair of MU trains occupy the storage tracks in front of the Gladstone on a Sunday afternoon in March 1984. The project to modify the catenary to allow operation of the next generation of commuter equipment is nearly complete, and all the supports have been repainted and their wire suspension and insulators have been changed.

Lower Right: The storage yard at the rural town of Gladstone was a particularly good location for photography of the former DL&W MU cars. With a little care in selective camera angles, the offset word "ERIE" on the cars letterboards could be masked to create a scene which might have existed in the 1930s, as this March 1984 view illustrates.

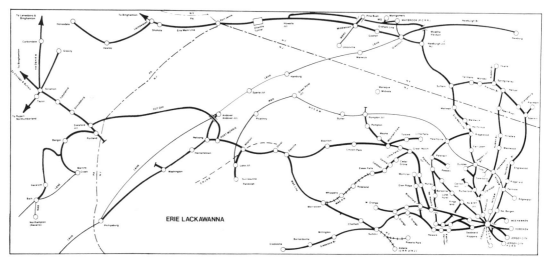

ERIE LACKAWANNA

Erie Lackawanna Employee Timetable #3, April 25, 1971

114

Above: Late on a Sunday evening in December 1980 the Gladstone yard is nearly full. The storage yard east of the station has a train on every track except the main, and the remaining space on the group of three tracks in front of the station will be taken by the last train of the evening. Thirteen #2 flashbulbs were used to illuminate the cluster of MU trains posed on the station tracks.

Upper Left: A two man effort was necessary to light this MU train at the west end of the Gladstone station leads and the residence across the street. Jim Boyd opened the camera shutters and illuminated the front of the train with a flashbulb before crossing the street to light up the house. The author worked from the rear of the MU train back toward the front, setting off a sequence of flashbulbs, and ending up back at the cameras to close the shutters.

Lower Left: Storm clouds sweep the sky at twilight as an MU coach waits on the storage track next to the station platform lead for the morning's commuter rush. Only the presence of a coach in the red and cream New Jersey Transit paint scheme, waiting on the lead behind the old bunkhouse in the background, reveals that the scene is in the 1980s rather than the 1960s or 1970s.

Overleaf: The last train of the evening has arrived at Gladsone on a Sunday in December 1980, and the yard is full. From the grade crossing between the station tracks and the storage yard, this view looks back at the station. Fifteen #2 flashbulbs set off with a hand-held reflector were used to light the scene, and the obvious flash positions in the foreground illustrate that it is possible to set off flashbulbs in the middle of a night scene without being illuminated by them.

Above: A series of flashbulbs set off with the camera shutter open illuminate the station, the parking lot, and the MU cars. By moving constantly during the process of setting off the flashbulbs, and by staying out of the area illuminated by the bulbs, no image of the photographer is recorded in the photo even though the lighting was done from near the center of the scene. A careful selection of flash angles avoids lighting another string of coaches on the track to the right of the group being photographed. Night shots are one of the few instances in outdoor photography where the photographer can totally control the illumination of the scene and take a completely creative approach to how the results will look.

Below: The Gladstone station is a delightful wooden structure with an elegance seldom seen in the more utilitarian designs of recent years. In the early 1980s, most of the lighting around the station was still incandescant bulbs, which lend their warm glow to the platform and the standing lines of MU cars.

EPILOGUE

The Erie Lackawanna was more than just a railroad, it was thousands of people trying to wrestle success out of an aging physical plant in an area of the country where the heavy industries, on which the railroads depend for their traffic, were already in serious trouble. The ultimate failure of the Erie Lackawanna was more devastating than can be conveyed by images of scraplines of elderly diesels, deserted buildings, torn up yards, and a trail of ballast through the weeds. The Erie Lackawanna was an organization of people, and many of them left the railroad industry forever. The shops that were closed and the yards that were torn up equated directly into a loss of jobs. Where such losses occured, it had a tremendous impact in the communities which the Erie Lackawanna served. Some of the towns and cities which were the locations of major facilities on the railroad have not fully recovered from the economic impact of the job losses more than ten years after the railroad ceased to exist.

Conrail maintains service to some parts of the old EL system, but it is notably tragic that Conrail had to be created at all. In the years since the demise of the EL some defendable arguments can be made, most of them with the benefit of nearly perfect hindsight, that different decisions by the Erie Lackawanna's management might have yielded more positive results, or perhaps greater flexibility and concessions by the rail unions might have changed the outcome. However, the principal influence in the decline and fall of the Erie Lackawanna seems to have been a failure of government policy relating to heavy industries in general and specifically to the rail transportation industry in the Northeast. The factors which seem to have had the greatest influence on the failure of the Erie Lackawanna were the bankruptcy laws, (which created a "house of cards" that toppled to financially strangle the smaller railroads in the area when the largest road, the Penn Central, encountered financial problems), an industry-wide regulation structure which hampered the performance of the railroads in the Northeast, and the trade laws which created a favorable environment for foreign competition, and eroded the industrial base on which the area railroads depended. In a season when concern over national competitiveness has suddenly become stylish, the failure of the Erie Lackawanna provides a poignant message: There is a high price to be paid for outdated regulatory structures and governmental indifference. Given similar inattentiveness on the part of government and industry, what happened to the Erie Lackawanna could just as easily happen anywhere, at any time, in any other American industry.

Above: After a Dayton train had backed across the AC interlocking plant in Marion, there was a few minutes for the crew to talk with the bystanders, read the evening paper, or even grab a take-along snack from the Depot Hotel Restaurant while the timers ran down the signals. With the typical power lashup headed by a freight converted E8, the crew on this Dayton train prepares to head out onto the branch on an evening in May 1973.

Upper Right: In 1973 the Erie Lackawanna initiated a caboose repaint and upgrade program at the Meadville, Pennsylvania car shops, which included the application of a colorful paint scheme which is based on the locomotive color scheme, but with the maroon and grey reversed. EL (ex-Erie) bay window caboose C315, on the Marion caboose tracks in August 1973, displays the attractive paint scheme.

Lower Right: Erie Lackawanna caboose C893 clatters westward across the diamonds at AC interlocking plant in Marion, Ohio, in October 1974. These very heavy cabooses, built by the Lackawanna railroad in the late 1940s at the Keyser Valley shops, were constructed on the underframes of tenders from the railroads retired fleets of Mikado and Pacific type steam locomotives. Because of the heavy underframes, they were favorites for use in areas where pushers might be used.

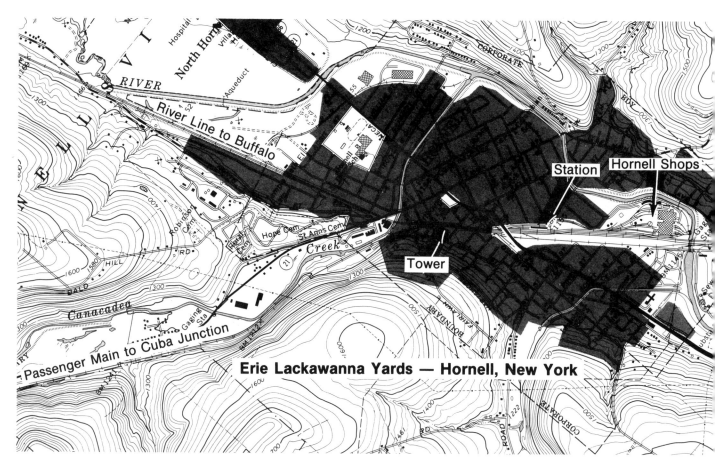

Erie Lackawanna Yards — Hornell, New York

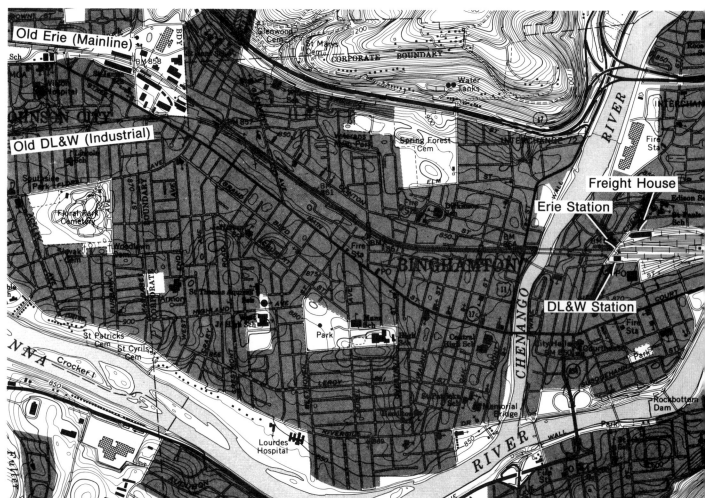

Crew Office

East Yard Throat

BM 1141

RIVER

South Horrell

U.S. Department of the Interior — Geological Survey

D&H to Belden Hill

D&H Bevier Street Yard

Popes Ravine

BINGHAMTON

Radio Towers (WINR)

EL Syracuse & Utica Branch

State Hospital

Ex-Erie now Conrail

ERIE-LACKAWANNA

SUSQUEHANNA

Temple Israel Riverside Cem

Filtration Plant

Conklin Yard

Ex-DL&W now D&H

Erie Lackawanna Yards — Binghamton, New York

125

ERIE LACKAWANNA RAILROAD
DIESEL LOCOMOTIVE ROSTER,
Compiled by Preston Cook

Group Road Noumbers	Quantity	Manufacturer	Model	Period Built	Previous Owner or Notes
19	1	AGEIR	Boxcab	1928	
26	1	GE	44 Ton	1946	Erie 26
51-53	3	GE	44 Ton	1948	DL&W 51-53
302-305	4	Alco	HH-660	1939	Erie 302-305
306-321	16	Alco	S1	1946-50	Erie 306-321
322,323	2	Alco	HH660	1933	DL&W 405,406
324,325	2	Alco	HH660	1940	DL&W 409,410
349-359	11	EMC	SW1	1940	DL&W 427-437
360	1	EMD	SW1	1948	Erie 360
361-371	11	EMD	SW8	1951-53	DL&W 501-511
381-385	5	BLW	DS44-660	1946-49	Erie 381-385
386-389	4	BLW	DS44-750	1949	Erie 386-389
401-403	3	EMC	NW2	1939	Erie 401-403
404-427	24	EMD	NW2	1948-49	Erie 404-427
428-433	6	EMD	SW7	1950	Erie 428-433
434-440	7	EMD	SW9	1951-52	Erie 434-440
441-445	5	EMD	NW2	1945	DL&W 461-465
446-455	10	EMD	SW9	1951-53	DL&W 551-560
456-463	8	EMD	SW1200	1957	DL&W 561-568
500-525	26	Alco	S2	1946-49	Erie 501-525
526-529	2	Alco	S4	1951-52	Erie 526-529
530-533	6	Alco	S2	1947	Erie 530-533
534-550	17	Alco	S2	1945-49	DL&W 475-491
600-616	17	BLW	DS44-1000	1946-49	Erie 600-616
617-628	12	BLW	S12	1951-52	Erie 617-628
650-659	10	Lima	1000HP	1949	Erie 650-659
660-665	6	Lima	1200HP	1950	Erie 660-665
801-803	3	EMD	SD45	1967	Owned by D&H
809	1	EMD	E8A	1951	DL&W 820
810-811	2	EMD	E8A	1951	DL&W 810,811 ex-Demo
812-819	8	EMD	E8A	1951	DL&W 812-819
820-833	14	EMD	E8A	1951	Erie 820-833
850-861	12	Alco	PA1	1949	Erie 850-861
862-863	2	Alco	PA2	1951	Erie 862-863
900-913	14	Alco	RS2	1949	Erie 900-913
914-933	20	Alco	RS3	1950-53	Erie 914-933
950-954	5	Alco	RS2	1949	Erie 950-954
1004	1	Alco	RS3	1950	Rebuild of D&H wreck
1005,1006	2	Alco	RS3	1950	Erie 1005,1006
1007-1038	32	Alco	RS3	1950-52	Erie 1007-1038
1039-1056	18	Alco	RS3	1950-52	DL&W 901-918
1057	1	Alco	RS3	Various	Built from 3 wrecks
1060	1	Alco	RS3M	1951	EL 1027, EMD engine
1061	1	Alco	RS3M	1952	EL 932, EMD engine
1101-1105	5	BLW	DRS44-1500	1949	Erie 1101-1105
1106-1120	15	BLW	AS16	1951-52	Erie 1106-1120
1140	1	BLW	AS16	1951	Erie 1140
1150-1161	12	BLW	DRS66-1500	1950	Erie 1150-1161
1200-1246	47	EMD	GP7	1950-52	Erie 1200-1246
1260-1265	6	EMD	GP9	1956	Erie 1260-1265
1270-1284	15	EMD	GP7	1951-52	DL&W 951-965
1400-1404	5	EMD	GP7P	1950-52	Erie 1400-1404
1405-1409	5	EMD	GP7P	1953	DL&W 966-970
1850-1859	10	FMC	H-24-66	1953	DL&W 850-859 (w/SG)
1860,1861	2	FMC	H-24-66	1956	DL&W 860,861 (no SG)
1930-1935	6	FMC	H-16-44	1952	DL&W 930-935
2001-2019	19	EMD	GP38-2	N/B	Order Cancelled
2301-2320	20	GE	U23B	N/D	Order Cancelled
2401-2415	15	Alco	C424	1963	
2451-2462	12	Alco	C425	1964	
2501-2527	27	GE	U25B	1964-65	
2551-2586	26	EMD	GP35	1964-65	
3301-3315	15	GE	U33C	1968-69	Dual control stands
3316-3327	12	GE	U36C	1972	
3601-3620	20	EMD	SD45	1967	
3621-3634	14	EMD	SD45	1968	Dual control stands
3635-3653	19	EMD	SDP45M	1969	Dual control stands
3654-3668	15	EMD	SDP45M	1970	
3669-3681	13	EMD	SD45-2	1972	
6011,6014	2	EMD	FTA	1945	DL&W 601A,601C
6012	1	EMD	FTB	1945	DL&W 601B
6021,6024	2	EMD	FTA	1945	DL&W 602A,602C
6022	1	EMD	FTB	1945	DL&W 602B
6031,6034	2	EMD	FTA	1945	DL&W 603A,603C
6032	1	EMD	FTB	1945	DL&W 603B
6041,6044	2	EMD	FTA	1945	DL&W 604A,604C
6042	1	EMD	FTB	1945	DL&W 604B
(—),6054	2	EMD	F3A	1946	DL&W 605A,605C
6052	1	EMD	F3B	1946	DL&W 605B
6061,6064	2	EMD	F3A	1946	DL&W 606A,606C
6062	1	EMD	F3B	1946	DL&W 606B
6111,6114	2	EMD	F7A	1949	DL&W 611A,611C
6112	1	EMD	F7B	1949	DL&W 611B
6211,6214	2	EMD	F3A	1948	DL&W 621A,621C
6212	1	EMD	F3B	1948	DL&W 621B

This list includes only units which were on the property or active during the lifetime of the Erie Lackawanna.

SG = Steam Generator; **N/B** = Not Built; **N/D** = Not Delivered; **EMC** = Electro-Motive Corporation, Subsidiary of GM;

EMD = Electro-Motive Division of General Motors Corporation; **Alco** = American Locomotive Company; **GE** = General Electric Company;

AGEIR = Alco/General Electric/Ingersol-Rand; **FMC** = Fairbanks Morse Company; **BLW** = Baldwin Locomotive Works

Group Road Numbers	Quantity	Manufacturer	Model	Period Built	Previous Owner or Notes
6311,6314	2	EMD	F7A	1949	DL&W 631A,631C
6321,6322	2	EMD	F7A,F7B	1949	DL&W 632A,632B
6331,6332	2	EMD	F7A,F7B	1949	DL&W 633A,633B
6341,6342	2	EMD	F7A,F7B	1949	DL&W 634A,634B
6351,6352	2	EMD	F7A,F7B	1949	DL&W 635A,635B
6361,6362	2	EMD	F7A,F7B	1949	DL&W 636A,636B
6511,6512	2	EMD	FTA,FTB	1945	DL&W 651A,651B
6521,6522	2	EMD	FTA,FTB	1945	DL&W 652A,652B
6531,6532	2	EMD	FTA,FTB	1945	DL&W 653A,653B
6541,6542	2	EMD	FTA,FTB	1945	DL&W 654A,654B
6551,6552	2	EMD	F3A,F3B	1947	DL&W 655A,655B
6561,6562	2	EMD	F3A,F3B	1947	DL&W 656A,656B
6571,6572	2	EMD	F3A,F3B	1948	DL&W 657A,657B
6581,6582	2	EMD	F3A,F3B	1948	DL&W 658A,658B
6591,6592	2	EMD	F3A,F3B	1948	DL&W 659A,659B
6601,6602	2	EMD	F3A,F3B	1948	DL&W 660A,660B
6611,6612	2	EMD	F3A,F3B	1948	DL&W 661A,661B
6621,6622	2	EMD	F3A,F3B	1948	DL&W 662A,662B
7001-7004	4	EMD	FT(ABBA)	1944	Erie 700A-700D
7011-7014	4	EMD	FT(ABBA)	1944	Erie 701A-701D
7021-7024	4	EMD	FT(ABBA)	1944	Erie 702A-702D
7031-7034	4	EMD	FT(ABBA)	1944	Erie 703A-703D
7041-7044	4	EMD	FT(ABBA)	1944	Erie 704A-704D
7051-7054	4	EMD	FT(ABBA)	1944	Erie 705A-705D
7061-7064	4	EMD	F3(ABBA)	1947	Erie 706A-706D
7071-7074	4	EMD	F3(ABBA)	1947	Erie 707A-707D
7081-7084	4	EMD	F3(ABBA)	1947	Erie 708A-708D
7091-7094	4	EMD	F3(ABBA)	1949	Erie 709A-709D
7101-7104	4	EMD	F3(ABBA)	1949	Erie 710A-710D
7111-7114	4	EMD	F7(ABBA)	1950	Erie 711A-711D
7121-7124	4	EMD	F7(ABBA)	1951	Erie 712A-712D
7131-7134	4	EMD	F7(ABBA)	1951	Erie 713A-713D
7141-7144	4	EMD	F7(ABBA)	1951-52	Erie 714A-714D
7251-7252	2	Alco	FA1,FB1	1947	Erie 725A, 725B
7253,7254	2	Alco	FB1,FA1	1947	Erie 725C,725D
7261,7262	2	Alco	FA1,FB1	1947	Erie 726A,726B
7263,7264	2	Alco	FB1,FA1	1947	Erie 726C,726D
7271,7272	2	Alco	FA1,FB1	1947	Erie 727A,727B
7273,7274	2	Alco	FB1,FA1	1947	Erie 727C,727D
7281,7282	2	Alco	FA1,FB1	1947	Erie 728A,728B
7283,7284	2	Alco	FB1,FA1	1947	Erie 728C,728D
7291,7292	2	Alco	FA1,FB1	1948	Erie 729A,729B
7293,7294	2	Alco	FB1,FA1	1948	Erie 729C,729D
7301,7302	2	Alco	FA1,FB1	1948	Erie 730A,730B
7303,7304	2	Alco	FB1,FA1	1948	Erie 730C,730D
7311,7312	2	Alco	FA1,FB1	1948	Erie 731A,731B
7313,7314	2	Alco	FB1,FA1	1948	Erie 731C,731D
7321,7322	2	Alco	FA1,FB1	1948	Erie 732A,732B
7323,7324	2	Alco	FB1,FA1	1948	Erie 732C,732D
7331,7332	2	Alco	FA1,FB1	1948	Erie 733A,733B
7333,7334	2	Alco	FB1,FA1	1948	Erie 733C,733D
7341,7342	2	Alco	FA1,FB1	1949	Erie 734A,345B
7343,7344	2	Alco	FB1,FA1	1949	Erie 734C,734D
7351,7352	2	Alco	FA1,FB1	1949	Erie 735A,735B
7353,7354	2	Alco	FB1,FA1	1949	Erie 735C,735D
7361,7362	2	Alco	FA2,FB2	1950	Erie 736A,736B
7363,7364	2	Alco	FB2,FA2	1950	Erie 736C,736D
7371,7372	2	Alco	FA2,FB2	1950	Erie 737A,737B
7373,7374	2	Alco	FB2,FA2	1950	Erie 737C,737D
7381,7382	2	Alco	FA2,FB2	1951	Erie 738A,738B
7383,7384	2	Alco	FB2,FA2	1951	Erie 738C,738D
7391,7392	2	Alco	FA2,FB2	1951	Erie 739A,739B
7393,7394	2	Alco	FB2,FA2	1951	Erie 739C,739D
8001,8004	2	EMD	F3A	1947	Erie 800A,800D
8002	1	EMD	F3B	1947	Erie 800B
8011,8014	2	EMD	F3A	1947	Erie 801A,801D
8012	1	EMD	F3B	1947	Erie 801B
8021,8024	2	EMD	F3A	1947	Erie 802A,802D
8022	1	EMD	F3B	1947	Erie 802B
8031,8034	2	EMD	F3A	1947	Erie 803A,803D
8032	1	EMD	F3B	1947	Erie 803B
8041,8044	2	EMD	F3A	1947	Erie 804A,804D
8042	1	EMD	F3B	1947	Erie 804B
8051,8054	2	EMD	F3A	1947	Erie 805A,805D
8052	1	EMD	F3B	1947	Erie 805B
8061,8064	2	EMD	F3A	1947	Erie 806A,806D
8062	1	EMD	F3B	1947	Erie 806B
8411,8414	2	EMD	F3A	1946	DL&W 801A,801C
8412	1	EMD	F3B	1946	DL&W 801B
8421,8424	2	EMD	F3A	1946	DL&W 802A,802C
8422	1	EMD	F3B	1944	DL&W 802B
8431,8434	2	EMD	F3A	1947	DL&W 803A,803C
8432	1	EMD	F3B	1947	DL&W 803B
8441,8444	2	EMD	F3A	1947	DL&W 804A,804C
8442	1	EMD	F3B	1947	DL&W 804B
8451,8454	2	EMD	F3A	1947	DL&W 805A,805C
8452	1	EMD	F3B	1947	DL&W 805B
3351-3373	23	GE	U34CH	1970-71	Owned by New Jersey DOT/ Operated by EL

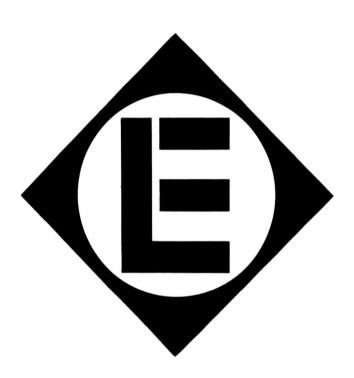